KINDER CONVERSATIONS

TALK IT OUT, WITHOUT FALLING OUT

TIM KEOGH

Copyright © 2022 by Tim Keogh

© A Kind Life Ltd 2022

ISBN13 Paperback: 979-8792578-66-1

ISBN13 Hardback: 978-1-913728-84-7

All rights reserved.

No part of this book may be reproduced in any form or by any electronic or mechanical means, including information storage and retrieval systems, without written permission from the author, except for the use of brief quotations in a book review.

CONTENTS

Part I
SETTING THE SCENE
1. Where It All Started — 7
2. Repairing Relationships — 13
3. The ABC of Appreciation — 16
4. If We Say Nothing, Nothing's Going to Change — 24

Part II
THE BUILD APPROACH
5. Introducing the BUILD Kinder Feedback Method — 35
6. Describe the Behaviour — 40
7. Understand Their Context — 43
8. Describe the Impact — 48
9. Facts or Feelings? — 50
10. Listen Up — 55
11. What Might You Do Differently? — 63
12. Putting It Into Action — 67

Part III
BUILD IN ACTION
13. All the Benefits of BUILD — 75
14. Talk to the Hand — 79
15. BUILD For Every Situation — 87
16. Speaking Up About Racism — 101

Part IV
MASTER BUILDER

17. Are You Receiving?   119
18. The Thing or Something Else?   126
19. The Best Storyteller You've Ever Met Is…   131
20. Moving Past the Fear of Giving Feedback   136
21. Serendipity   144

References   147

PART I

SETTING THE SCENE

1

WHERE IT ALL STARTED

We pulled into the driveway after our holiday, excited to catch up with our teenage kids, share stories and photographs from our trip, and to hear what they had been up to. At least, we were excited until we got in the house and saw the state of the kitchen.

A Leaning Tower of Pisa, made entirely of dirty dishes and pizza boxes, greeted us. My heart sank, and red-hot anger rose in its place. When the kids got home a couple of hours later, how do you suppose the conversation went?

If you guessed that I tore into them with both barrels about the dishes, you're right. "You are a disgrace. You're a real disappointment. You're so self-centred. You never think about other people!"

Voices were raised.
Doors were slammed.
Relationships were damaged.
Unhappy memories were made.

We all have moments when someone's behaviour is very different from what we hoped. And how do most of us react? In the case of unwashed dishes, you might attack, like I did. Shout, slam doors, or make a sarcastic remark. Or you might avoid the situation by saying nothing but quietly simmering about it. Perhaps you passive-aggressively wash the dishes yourself, banging pots around loudly so they can hear you.

But what if it didn't have to be this way? What if there was a way to have difficult conversations with ease? Think about what a difference that would make to your relationships, both at work and at home.

All this is possible, when you learn to give kinder feedback.

We all find ourselves in situations where we simply don't know how to give feedback without creating more friction. Perhaps your boss likes to add a stack of work to your desk at three pm on a Friday, and you don't know how to broach the subject. Perhaps your senior colleague is always putting you down. Or perhaps you have a friend who always jumps in with unwanted advice before you can finish your sentence, and you're not certain how to politely ask them to stop.

Perhaps you haven't thought about conversations in terms of giving feedback. We often approach conversations with the aim of making our point. We want to be right. We want to win the argument. We're looking for that self-righteous sense of scoring the point. We aren't thinking of the conversation as a collaboration where we give feedback to the other person, to hear their views and find a way forward together. We certainly don't think that they might want to give us feedback!

We aren't taught the skill of kinder feedback. I know I wasn't. I was taught to say what I feel - I'm just getting my retaliation in early - or to let it go, say nothing and simmer. Speaking up would only make it worse.

In short, I was taught to veer, as many of us do, between anger and avoidance.

But as I finished up the dishes, I started to think: about the arguments with the kids; about fractious work relationships; about unspoken unhappiness with family and friends… And I started to wonder, there has to be a better way, doesn't there?

My work is in culture change. Over the past ten years, I've helped more than fifty organisations around the world build kinder cultures. And I started to think that I wasn't exactly walking the walk here.

So, I determined to find a way to make it easier for people to reclaim these difficult conversations. What if there were a way to talk things out without falling out? A way to speak up without clamming up, to stop molehills of disagreement from becoming mountains of discord.

So over the next year I developed, piloted, and then refined my approach with thousands of people in hundreds of workshops.

The result was the Kinder Feedback Method, and the BUILD model that underpins it. You'll find BUILD to be the kindest and safest way to give and receive feedback.

Now is the time to learn to resolve concerns before they become issues - to turn mountains back into molehills. As you turn the page, you'll start learning the basics of the Kinder Feedback Method:

- How to use the ABCs of appreciation to nurture stronger relationships
- Why it's vital to speak up when we need to
- The BUILD kinder feedback framework and how to use it
- How to start important conversations on the right foot

- The secret of empathetic listening
- Moving from what's wrong to what would be better instead
- How to dig deeper and find what's really getting in the way
- Learning to receive feedback as a gift
- Retelling your story to reclaim your emotions
- Overcoming your fear of giving feedback

The heart of the Kinder Feedback Method is giving fearlessly gentle feedback with the BUILD model. Looking back, this approach to kinder feedback could have led to a very different outcome when I came home to the leaning tower of pizzas.

Since that moment, I've supported tens of thousands of people in high pressure environments like healthcare, education and tech. Doctors, nurses, managers, mothers, fathers, software developers, teachers, psychotherapists, administrators, chief executives, friends, siblings, lecturers, students, children, and mediators have all used these techniques to transform their teams, have better conversations, and create kinder cultures. And they've not only strengthened their working relationships, but their personal ones too, using kinder feedback to build flourishing families and friendships.

Like them, you can learn to:

- Tackle issues before they boil over into problems

- Give feedback in a productive way, both at work and home
- Feel more confident having conversations that you might previously have worried about

I use these techniques regularly too. They have transformed my relationships and results at work and at home. Being able to talk things out with ease and grace is essential to every relationship, everywhere.

This book will teach you these valuable approaches so you can change your conversations and revitalise your relationships. Are you ready to learn to give feedback without the fear, the friction, or the fallout? Let's begin.

2

REPAIRING RELATIONSHIPS

Relationships. Our lives are built on them. From our partners, to our colleagues, to the regular barista in our favourite coffee shop, our days are filled with human interactions.

The quality of our relationships has a powerful impact on our lives. If you have a good relationship with your co-workers, you're more likely to enjoy your work. You've got a better chance of achieving the results you want. If you live with a partner, a strong relationship makes for a happy and supportive home life. Good friendships and relationships help you thrive and reach the goals that matter to you.

Did you know, great relationships have a bigger impact on our life expectancy than what we eat or drink, and whether we smoke or exercise?[1] They're more important than money or success. A 70-year Harvard study found that having three or four great friendships (including friendships with your partner, a colleague, a sibling or a pal) is the greatest predictor of lifelong happiness.[2]

But relationships are easy when the going is good. It's when relationships get rocky that the rubber hits the road. It's when things are sticky that kindness makes the most difference. Yet this is when it's hardest to find the words.

Our partner refuses to help with a kitchen chore because, "That's your job - I take care of the laundry!" Or a friend falls into the habit of expecting you to pay every time you go out to eat together, and doesn't offer to get the bill sometimes. Maybe our uncle who never approved of our life choices starts ranting at us on every visit.

So, we bite our lip and say nothing. But if we say nothing, nothing changes. We might become resentful or frustrated, but starting a conversation without creating conflict can feel like trying to do a jigsaw puzzle in the dark.

The Kinder Feedback Method helps you have conversations when it matters most. Like any skill, this gets easier the more you practise it. As you grow in confidence, you'll find that improving one relationship has a ripple effect. You'll feel more at ease giving feedback in many situations, and you'll have smoother, more helpful conversations across the board.

Pause now and think about a relationship you need to have a conversation in. It might be with a colleague, a partner, a friend, or a family member. Pick something that isn't a big issue to start with, something that is a little annoying rather than deeply distressing. A four or five out of ten.

Maybe your colleague insists on dropping by your desk and interrupting your work instead of emailing. Maybe your teenager spends family meals glued to their phone even when asked to put it down, just for dinner. Or perhaps your partner keeps forgetting that the laundry basket exists and dumps their dirty clothes on the floor at the end of the bed.

WE'LL CALL THIS YOUR CHOSEN CONVERSATION.

What's stopping you from having the conversation you need to have? Is it fear of messing things up, or of the other person's reactions? Perhaps you've already tried and it didn't work out well.

How would it feel if you could have that conversation without friction or falling out? Take a moment to think about how things might be easier, happier, closer, and more productive, if you could.

As you read this book, I'll walk you through applying the Kinder Feedback Method to your Chosen Conversation.

When you change the conversation, you revitalise your relationships.

The Kinder Feedback Method helps you build the great relationships you deserve, in all aspects of your life.

3

THE ABC OF APPRECIATION

You might expect the Kinder Feedback Method to be all about speaking up when things are going wrong, yet the most powerful feedback is not critical feedback at all, but appreciative feedback. Praise. Letting them know what they did right.

Think about a time you felt appreciated. Perhaps your manager thanked you for sorting out a last-minute task, or your partner appreciated your thoughtfulness in getting dinner started when they were late home, or your mum loved that you remembered her favourite flowers on her birthday.

It feels good, doesn't it?

Appreciation is a founding principle of the Kinder Feedback Method. Appreciation helps to build happy, strong relationships. A study of 130 newly-wed couples found that only those who said they were in a happy marriage experienced five times more positive interactions than negative.[1]

When we appreciate each other, our relationships grow. Romantic relationships feel revitalised, friendships feel like an equal exchange, and, of course, appreciation plays a huge role in our working life.

In our Kinder Culture workshops, we ask attendees to remember the most important good day at work they can. A day so good that if all days were like that, they'd be able to more consistently do the amazing work they aspire to.

I've asked more than 30,000 professionals this question. What is the number one thing that makes the best workday they can remember? You guessed it: Appreciation. Gratitude. A simple 'thank you'.

Studies back this up: 78% of people would work harder if they were recognised.[2] One survey showed that an appreciative boss is worth a 13% pay rise.[3] When we feel appreciated at work, we perform better and are less likely to look for another job.

If you are a manager at work, do you want to hold on to your great team members? 79% of people who leave their job cite lack of appreciation as a key factor.[4] And 80% of people who feel appreciated are not actively looking for another job.[5]

Chidi was frustrated because his team was constantly grumbling. He'd catch them muttering in the break room, but clamming up as soon as he walked in. Chidi believed in motivation by offering advice about what to do better – but he never stopped to appreciate what was already going well. Using the ABCs of Appreciation (which you'll learn in a minute), Chidi got into the habit of appreciating his team. Morale went up and his relationship with his team improved.

How long does it take to appreciate someone? Well, in one group of NHS support staff I was working with, I asked them, "How long does it take to give positive feedback?"

Nigel, at the back of the room, folded his arms and shouted out, "Sixteen years!"

Can you imagine waiting that long for a simple thank you? Let's start showing appreciation to the people in our lives! All it takes is a moment. And it costs nothing.

Effective appreciation is genuine appreciation.

Genuine appreciation isn't a manager swanning into the room and saying, "You're all fabulous, good job." Vague, patronising rubbish doesn't stir people to action.

Genuine appreciation means noticing the little things, the specifics. Maybe the receptionist smiled and was kind when you arrived late and frazzled, or the cleaner in your office did a lovely job of the restroom. Maybe a nurse on your team held the hand of an anxious patient. Now the feedback you give is authentic, because the other person knows you noticed them specifically. It lifts their mood and builds confidence.

When Chidi learned about appreciation, he knew not to settle for a vague 'thanks, folks' at every team meeting. He turned things around by praising specific actions his team had taken. "Sandra, you handled that upset customer so well… Michael, thanks for going out of your way to finish that report early… Lisette, I appreciate that you took the time to help Jacinta understand our new software."

When people know they're doing the right thing, they're more likely to do it again. That's why appreciation is the number one driver of performance and behaviour change. Studies have shown that people in successful organisations, teams, families, and personal relationships receive up to five times as much positive feedback as critical feedback.[6]

THE BENEFITS OF APPRECIATION

Praise has many benefits. People at work feel more committed to their job, and people in relationships feel much happier. This counts for friendships too. When you show appreciation, people are more likely to seek an ongoing friendship with you.[7]

Ready to give appreciative feedback? It's easy when you remember your ABCs.

THE A B C OF APPRECIATION

A — ACTION
THIS IS WHAT YOU SAID OR DID

B — BENEFIT
THE POSITIVE IMPACT IT HAD

C — CONTINUE
THANKS, PLEASE KEEP DOING THIS

Action. Describe the specific thing the person said or did. Get past vague generalisations to the behaviour that you saw. Practise by noticing all the wonderful little things the people around you do every day. The A builds confidence because they know they are doing the right thing. It lifts their mood, and it makes the feedback authentic, because you took the time to notice them.

And that's a great start, but it's not enough on its own.

Benefit. Tell them the positive impact they had on you, someone else, the project, or the world. People often don't see the impact they're having – so show them. The B drives engagement and motivation by connecting our actions with the difference we are making.

Continue. Leave the other person in no doubt you'd like to see more of this. "Thanks, keep it up." Perhaps you'll say, "That's living up to our values," or, "You'll make a great nurse if you keep doing things this way." The C is the reinforcement. It builds confidence and consolidates the behaviour change.

WHAT NOT TO APPRECIATE

Not all appreciation is created equal. Don't praise:

Outcomes. When we praise outcomes, people find it hard to link the praise to their specific actions. Their results can actually get worse over time. Instead of, "Well done for winning that badminton game," try, "Your serve technique was perfect; it really strengthened your game!" Instead of, "Congratulations on landing that client," try, "You really explained our product perfectly, which swayed their decision to choose us." This 'process praise' suggests to people they can develop their abilities, and how they might do this.

Talent. Studies show that talent is a myth. Genuine world class performances in the arts or sports don't take talent. They take motivation, practice and coaching. Studies show that when we praise ability, people are more likely to display a helpless response to any set-backs. Their performance can get worse over time.[8] Instead look for the actions, skills or the practice they put in, and praise that. Instead of, "You're a natural at facilitating a group," try, "The way you gave everyone time to speak helped that group run smoothly."

Instead of telling your child, "You're so clever," try, "That study schedule you set up really helped you improve your grades."

A NOTE OF CAUTION

Appreciation drives behaviour change because it gives people a boost of endorphins, the feel-good hormone, which lifts their mood. It also floods the system with serotonin – our social hormone – so they're more likely to repeat the action.

For managers, that means driving performance. For parents, it's an invaluable way to encourage the behaviours they want to see from their children. In relationships, it reinforces the behaviours that create meaningful connection.

That sounds positive, so why the caution? Because it's very easy to focus only on what works for us. That's a natural human response – we want to make our life smoother. But it's important to be mindful of what is the best outcome for your team member, child, partner or colleague. If you're only appreciating what helps you meet your goals, or what makes your life easier, that could be a tiny bit manipulative.

When using the ABCs, always consider, "What is the best outcome for both of us?"

One final benefit of appreciation is that it builds such a strong foundation for a relationship it makes it easier to talk out issues when difficulties do appear. Studies show that people in appreciative relationships – at home, with friends, and at work – are much more open to receiving critical feedback and much better at working through concerns.[9] That's the magic of appreciating the people in your life.

Appreciation is one of the most powerful communication skills you can use, at work and at home, to have more good days and build better relationships.

So, think now about your Chosen Conversation. How could you use the ABCs to appreciate this person who is so important to you? Get specific and remember to appreciate actions, not talents or outcomes.

4

IF WE SAY NOTHING, NOTHING'S GOING TO CHANGE

It was a bright autumn morning. Seventy-two neonatal intensive care clinicians were heading into work, a little more relaxed than usual as today was a training day... and what they thought was an exercise in team working.

But it wasn't. In fact, it was a blind study on the impact of rudeness at work.[1] Working in groups of three, they were told an expert in teamwork would observe them and comment on how they were doing. For half of the groups, the expert made comments in a completely neutral tone. The other half got mildly unkind comments. The expert didn't question their work at all, but simply used an uncivil tone of voice.

The results?

The teams exposed to rudeness made errors – significantly more errors in diagnosis and significantly more errors in the execution of clinical procedures. It wasn't even the words the expert spoke that made the difference, just the tone. Think about that for a moment.

Incivility isn't just mean. Hearing it means we are more likely to make mistakes. And we've all been there: your boss was overbearing, your teammate was cutting corners, your partner's been snippy all afternoon. But did you say anything? Probably not. Most of us just let things go. Why? We're scared of their reactions (speaking up will make things worse) or of the repercussions (getting in trouble with the boss). Or maybe we think, "They're just like that, they'll never change."

I developed the BUILD model over twelve months of practising, refining and honing with more than 1,000 people, and in the past ten years, I've shared and practised and refined BUILD with many thousands more. Together, we have created an easy, structured way to start these vital conversations.

BUILD is a cornerstone of the Kinder Feedback Method. It's the kindest, safest, easiest and quickest way to give feedback. It's the kindest, safest, easiest and quickest way to receive feedback too.

IF YOU SAY NOTHING NOTHING CHANGES

Let me tell you a story about Grace. Grace was in her 80s and was recovering in hospital after an operation. Grace found most of the team lovely but there was one nurse she described as "a bit grumpy." When Grace asked for a glass of water, this nurse sighed and muttered sharply that she was busy. She brought the water – with another big sigh.

Grace mentioned it to another nurse who told her, "Don't worry, she's just like that sometimes."

Later, when Grace needed to go to the bathroom and only the 'grumpy' nurse was around, Grace didn't want to be a bother. She waited until she was desperate enough to try and take herself to the restroom. Grace fell trying to get out of bed and broke her hip.

Thanks to the great staff in that hospital, Grace made a full recovery, but perhaps the outcome would have been different if the second nurse had spoken with her occasionally grumpy colleague.

In our Kinder Culture workshops, we have asked 30,000 professionals what makes a bad day at work for them. They were people in high pressure environments like healthcare, education and technology. For more than two-thirds of people, bad days at work are caused by colleagues' poor behaviour, ranging from incivility, rudeness, shouting, tutting, eye rolling, aggressive grumpiness, and gossip, to full on bullying.

This is the real rich tapestry of incivility at work. And of course, it's not pleasant to experience. But what impact does it have? What happens when we are on the receiving end of this behaviour?

When we are on the end of what we perceive as rudeness, it's a threat, a threat to life, just as if there were a tiger in the room. We go into the survival mode, developed over hundreds of thousands of years to keep us safe, called fight or flight. Our brain wants us to fight or flee.

You may have heard of fight or flight, but did you know there are three Fs in fight or flight? The third F is *freeze*. We go completely still, hoping the tiger might mistake us for a tree and stroll on by.

When we perceive ourselves as being on the receiving end of rudeness, it activates our fight or flight response. 10% of the blood from your brain drains into your body, ready to run or attack. This reduces cognitive function, and evidence shows that reduced function harms memory, decision-making ability, and creativity.

So, by the time the other person walks away, you're not thinking about what you were doing before. You're angry and distracted. This isn't a good outcome.

In another healthcare study, this time in New York, a series of anaesthetists were faced with a clinical simulation that, intentionally, went horribly wrong.[2] They were tasked with working as a surgical team to sort the situation out. But the surgeon in the simulation was a plant. To half of the participants the surgeon was polite, kind and encouraging. To the other half he was rude, impatient and aggressive. The anaesthetists with the polite surgeon reached 91% of expected performance. Those with the rude surgeon, only 63%. That's a massive difference in performance. And in healthcare, that's going to make a big difference to patient safety, and quality of patient outcomes.

Rudeness at work has wide-ranging consequences. It makes mistakes more likely, breaks down teamwork, and harms productivity. Incivility in families leads to damaged relationships, a tense home atmosphere, and a lack of healthy communication. And – as we will discuss later – discrimination harms individuals and communities.

Rudeness is contagious. If someone is rude to you, then you are more likely to be rude to others. Makes sense, doesn't it? We've all had moments when we snapped at our partner or friend because our boss was obnoxious to us.

You may be thinking, "I get this, but that's not me. When people are mean I'm aware of what's going on. I don't react in this way." Well – back to our anaesthetists. After the study, participants were asked if they had the polite surgeon or the rude surgeon, and they all got it right; they recognised the behaviour. They were then asked if they felt it had harmed their performance. And they all said it had not. "I'm a professional; this kind of thing doesn't affect me." But it did. And it affects you too.

So, what happens if we don't give feedback? If we just walk on by?

The person who did something harmful will probably not know the impact they had so they are likely to keep doing it. They don't have the chance to reflect, learn and change so they continue harming you, others, safety and quality.

Slowly, this kind of behaviour becomes the norm. Our norm. And by ignoring our standards, we are setting new, lower standards for all of those around us in our relationships, our family or our team.

In the next chapter I'll introduce you to our Kinder Feedback Method, BUILD. By learning to use BUILD, you are literally helping everyone around you to improve their quality of work, their quality of life, and the quality of their relationships.

And we need to say something, because, as we have seen, if we say nothing, nothing changes.

But our natural inclination is not to speak up kindly. We go into fight or flight. We attack or avoid. Which of these are you more likely to do?

I used to attack. My preferred attack weapon was to question motives: "What on earth did you do that for?... Well, what did you think was going to happen?"

Maybe yours is sarcasm: "Well, that was clever, wasn't it?" Or name calling: "You idiot (or worse)." Maybe you attack with direct orders: "Don't do that! Do what I told you to."

Or you go straight for their personality traits: "You're such a mean, nasty person." Some of us question intentions: "You must really hate me to do that."

In short, you tell the person off. It might feel better in the moment. It might even drive short term change if you're in a position of power. But they'll get defensive and emotional in response. At work, people will reduce their effort. At home, it builds resentment. In friendships, it creates distance. It doesn't help long term.

Or maybe you avoid? You seethe in silence, mutter comments under your breath, or stamp around passive-aggressively.

So, think for a moment about your Chosen Conversation, and the behaviour that's led up to this point. Consider how you have reacted up to now. Do you tend to attack? Or do you avoid? What was the outcome of those responses? Was it helpful?

Of course, neither of these reactions means you're a bad person. We're simply not taught how to have conversations we perceive as difficult.

Until now.

So, head to the next chapter and I'll introduce you to BUILD, and the Kinder Feedback Method.

PART II

THE BUILD APPROACH

5

INTRODUCING THE BUILD KINDER FEEDBACK METHOD

In this chapter, I'll introduce you to the BUILD Kinder Feedback Method that we have developed, refined, and proven with tens of thousands of people just like you.

BUILD removes that sense of difficulty so we can move past the issue and towards a resolution. At work, things will be safer, teams more productive, and results better. At home, relationships will be closer, more rewarding and fun. And in our friendships, we'll understand each other better, have a more balanced relationship, and communicate more clearly. BUILD helps to build solutions, to build relationships, to build trust.

BUILD is an acronym that stands for:

- Describe the **Behaviour**
- **Understand** their context
- Describe the **Impact**
- **Listen** to them
- Ask, "What might you / we do **Differently**?"

You can see BUILD is similar to the ABC of appreciation.

The B stands for Behaviour. Tell them the behaviour you observed. It's similar to the A for Action in ABC.

The I stands for Impact. It's like the B in the ABC. But this is likely to be a negative impact rather than a benefit.

Unlike the ABC, we don't want them to continue the behaviour. So instead of the C (continue) we have D – what can we do differently?

But, "You did this; the impact was that; do something differently," sounds a bit like a telling-off, doesn't it?

So, I added two steps.

U stands for Understand. With as much empathy as you can muster, understand for a moment what the other person might be going through. Step into their shoes. The U is unsaid. Just imagine, with some generosity, what the other person might be going through.

And L stands for Listen. Let them explain their point of view. Hear their side of the story. These two additional steps turn BUILD feedback into a dialogue, a discussion.

Let me introduce you to Sally. Sally works in a hospital administration team. She'd learned about BUILD in a workshop the previous morning and had a chance to practise it that afternoon. She wanted to tell us how it had worked for her.

Sally was able to resolve a situation that would previously have ended very differently.

"A senior doctor called to chase some notes," Sally told us. "He was angry, really shouting. It was upsetting."

The first step in BUILD is to describe the Behaviour, without emotion or judgement. It is just a factual statement of what's happening. Sally did this by taking a deep breath and saying,

"You have really raised your voice." Before BUILD, she might have chosen more emotional words: "You're shouting at me when I'm only trying to help you! Your attitude is only making the situation worse." Would this have worked? Would it have de-escalated the situation? No. The consultant would likely have got more irritated or even slammed the phone down. But with BUILD, Sally was able to describe the behaviour without judgement.

The second step is Understanding. It was easy to see this doctor was most likely under a lot of pressure and probably needed the notes to treat a patient – perhaps urgently.

Sally described the Impact. When the senior staff member raised his voice to her, Sally calmly told him, "I can't concentrate on what you're saying."

After she explained that the other person's raised voice was making it hard to understand what they were saying, Sally moved on to the next step of BUILD: Listening.

Sally asked, "What's happening here?" That question opened a dialogue. Her colleague told her, "I need those files so I can treat a patient who needs urgent care. But I can see that shouting at you isn't going to help." He calmed down a little, and they were able to come up with a plan together.

So, what happened after Sally used the B-U-I-L of BUILD? Her colleague called her back later to apologise. Sally took the opportunity to finish BUILD with the D – "What might you do differently?"

He told her he realised he'd been shouting at a lot of people and was going to have a think about it. I later heard that this person had a reputation for his fiery temper, but that he'd changed a lot. And all it took was being walked through the five simple steps of BUILD by a colleague.

He didn't know Sally was using the BUILD framework (you don't have to announce it every time you use it), but her non-judgemental statements and strong listening skills were enough to create some self-awareness and change.

BUILD is a conversation, not an argument. With BUILD, you can be confident to speak up without clamming up, whether at work, at home, or out in the world.

Now you've seen BUILD in action, think about your Chosen Conversation.

Can you imagine what it would be like if you used BUILD instead? What would be the impact on your life if you could have that conversation in a kinder and more productive way that moved the relationship beyond the issue?

Let's start work on that together now...

6

DESCRIBE THE BEHAVIOUR

Let's go back to the leaning tower of pizza plates that I described in the introduction. As I started to teach BUILD I used this as an example with one group to work out what I could have said to get a better outcome.

Picture the scene. A week's worth of pizza boxes, dirty dishes, mouldering mugs.

We start our BUILD feedback by describing the other person's behaviour. So instead of our original pre-BUILD reactions, attacking or avoiding, we need to describe what they did, factually and without judgements.

I asked the group whether it would be fair to say, "You've left the kitchen in a mess?"

"Perhaps not," one of them suggested. "I've seen a lot worse than this. At least those plates look neatly stacked around the sink."

So 'mess' is my interpretation, my judgement. It's not a fact. If someone can disagree then it's a judgement. Your beliefs and feelings are not facts, no matter how strongly you believe them.

After talking it through for a few minutes we agreed on: "There are lots of dirty plates around the sink."

The group were having fun by this time. "You think that's lots? I already did half of it!" So even 'lots' is a little judgemental.

We agreed to describe the behaviour like this: "There are dirty plates in the sink."

You can imagine a sullen teenager at this point shrugging with a sullen 'yeah'.

But that's great. They may not like to hear it, but they have to agree it's true. And agreement is the perfect place to start a conversation. That's what the behaviour step is all about – starting the conversation from a point of agreement. It's so much better, I think you can agree, than starting from a point of disagreement.

So, with BUILD we start by describing behaviours as facts.

We need to be mindful of using judgemental words when having these conversations.

If, as you start to describe the behaviour, you hear yourself say, "you are" then alarm bells should start ringing. "You are" means a judgement is coming.

Remember my original reaction to the dirty dishes. "You are a disgrace. You're a real disappointment. You are so self-centred; you never think about other people."

These are judgements. They describe judgements or personality traits, not behaviours.

What would you say if someone told you that you were lazy or thoughtless, mean or rude? Most likely you'd fire back with an indignant, "Excuse me? I'm no such thing!"

Judgements put the person on the defensive. They're much more likely to disagree with your assessment of them. "You are…" is the perfect way to start an argument.

"You did" is a much kinder way to start feedback and find a resolution.

Your aim in giving feedback is not to win. Your aim is to find a resolution, to open up space for your colleague, or kid or loved one to learn and change. And you start this by describing what they did as facts, not interpretations; as truths not judgements; as behaviours not personality traits.

Think about your Chosen Conversation. If you were to describe the other person's behaviour without judgement, what might you say?

You can pause here to write down some ideas if you like.

7

UNDERSTAND THEIR CONTEXT

The second step of BUILD is understanding. Just take a moment to understand their perspective, with a generous dash of generosity and empathy.

Seeing things from their point of view goes a long way to smoothing over sticky situations.

But Tim, you might say, how can I know what they're thinking or feeling? You can't. And the aim here isn't to correctly guess their thoughts or emotions. You'll probably never know. This is about exercising your empathy and softening your sense of indignation.

U also stands for unsaid. You don't say anything aloud. Just imagine it in your own head and let that empathy guide you into kinder feedback.

The U step of BUILD is based on the word of Edward de Bono. De Bono was a Maltese physician and psychologist who coined the term 'lateral thinking'.

De Bono used a tool called OPS (Other People's Shoes). He was asked to visit a mine in South Africa, where there were ninety fist fights a month between co-workers. You can imagine that a mine is a pretty hellish place to work at the best of times. Add in constant physical fights, and it gets a lot worse. Workers would get into serious scuffles, which made for an even more unsafe and unpleasant working environment.

De Bono taught the mine workers OPS so they could practise stepping into the other person's shoes. When two workers were about to fall out because Jay thought Kai was shirking his duty, De Bono taught them to use OPS. Jay figured that maybe Kai was just tired or hungry. And Kai wondered if Jay was worried about his family; maybe one of his kids was ill.

And just by teaching workers OPS, the number of fights dropped by 85%. That's the power of a little empathy.

As humans, we're great storytellers. No matter the situation, we're always telling our own story about it. The problem comes when we project our own story onto the other person, instead of trying to understand their context.

For example, our boss snaps at us when we try to present a new idea. So, we assume that our boss is a) an ass and b) doesn't care about our ideas. But in fact, they were already fifteen minutes late to an important meeting because their cat threw up and then their car broke down.

And if you're thinking, "I couldn't have known that," of course you're right. But by projecting our own story onto the other person, we're adding aggravation that isn't based on fact either. We're mad with the boss for hating ideas – before we know whether or not they actually did.

By taking a breather and letting ourselves imagine a more generous explanation than the judgemental one we've created, we're leaving room for empathy.

When I was developing BUILD I put the U between the B and the I so it spells BUILD, which is easy to remember. But you can move this step around. Sometimes it's better to do this first before you start to give feedback.

Empathy is a learned skill. The more you practise it the better you'll get. Before a tense situation really kicks off, step into the other person's shoes and think about what might be happening for them. Maybe a family member is sick. Maybe they're struggling to pay the rent. Maybe they're worried about the redundancies that have been announced.

Now you're starting out from a place focused not on winning but on understanding.

There's a saying that sympathy is stepping into someone else's shoes, but empathy means taking off your own shoes first. That means dropping your assumptions, judgements and disappointments first, then you think about their point of view with a clearer head.

Thinking about my kids and the dirty plates, I wonder now if maybe they were going to do it but overslept or got carried away in a game or movie.

This takes a certain amount of generosity. It doesn't make what they've done right, and it doesn't take away the need for a behavioural change. But it does change the nature and quality of the conversation.

Engaging your empathy affects how you approach important conversations. It changes your tone of voice, which is much more important than you might realise.

A study in healthcare showed that the single most important factor in whether a patient makes a formal complaint about their experience is the tone of voice that the clinician uses when talking with the patient. Not the months of waiting; not the outcome of the surgery; not the words they use: just their tone.

When our thought process is, "I'm so angry; this person obviously hates me," it has an effect on the way we speak to them. But if we swap that for, "Perhaps there's something going on with them – maybe they're having a bad day," our voice gets a little kinder and gentler.

Think again about the person you want to have your Chosen Conversation with. Conjure up that person and situation in your mind. Step into their shoes for a moment and consider what might be going on for them. What might be happening? What pressures might they be under? What past hurt might be contributing to their current behaviour?

How might your response to them be different now you've thought about it from their perspective?

8

DESCRIBE THE IMPACT

The third step in BUILD is describing the impact the behaviour is having. You are describing how the behaviour harmed something. How it impacted the team, the project, the relationship, or how it made you feel.

This becomes easier once you have stepped into their shoes and you can approach the conversation with understanding.

When was the last time you stopped mid-conversation to wonder how you were landing with the other person and what impact you were having? We're not taught to do that. The I step in BUILD helps the other person see the impact of their behaviour.

In the introduction, I told you about a sink full of dirty dishes, and how my immediate response was to tell my kids what I thought of their behaviour. Using BUILD I could have described the impact clearly so we could move forward.

In Behaviours we talked about the importance of separating facts from feelings. In the I step of BUILD, you can own how the behaviour made you feel – and that's fine. For example, I might have said, "That felt disrespectful to me, and has put a dark cloud at the end of what was a lovely holiday."

In this way, you can use BUILD to help the other person understand the practical and emotional impact of their behaviour.

Jamila had a friend who liked a good bit of banter, but sometimes it felt a little mean-spirited. It felt less like banter and more like they were insulting Jamila's life choices.

Using BUILD Jamila was able to describe the impact of their behaviour: "This banter makes me feel like you don't respect my ability to make choices about my own life."

Notice Jamila didn't say, "You're being cruel and you don't care about my feelings." That would be a judgement on her friend's feelings and perception. She kept the focus on the impact – on her own feelings. She didn't assume her friend's intent. With BUILD Jamila felt she could speak up without messing up. They could move beyond the issue to a resolution.

Think of your Chosen Conversation. How might you describe the impact of their behaviour on you, on your feelings, and on your relationship?

9

FACTS OR FEELINGS?

As you now understand, it is perfectly ok to talk about your feelings in the Impact step of BUILD. But in the Behaviour step it is important to stick only to the facts. So, let's dive a little deeper into this before we explore the last two steps of BUILD.

Kinder feedback involves finding kinder words. Separating facts from feelings helps you have these kinder conversations.

When you give kinder feedback you:

Separate what they did from what you felt about it.

Separate the reality from your judgement of it.

Separate their behaviours from their personality traits.

Separate what objectively happened from your subjective view of the situation.

KINDER CONVERSATIONS

We're taught as children to judge people. And these judgements aren't always kind.

Maybe you heard your parents saying your new friend is a waste of space, your great aunt is a weirdo or your cousin doesn't have the sense God gave a goose.

We are taught to stick labels onto people. But these labels are judgements. They are feelings, not objective facts. With BUILD we remove the labels. We separate facts from feelings.

Here's an example taken from an unexpected moment of BUILD in action.

I was presenting the BUILD concept to the leadership team of a large NHS organisation. Almost immediately, one of the attendees started cutting into my presentation to make their own points. We only had thirty minutes, so I was worried that I might not be able to cover all the key points. Also, other attendees were finding it unsettling.

Right, I thought. Here's a great opportunity for people to experience BUILD in action. After all, it's not every day I get the chance to demonstrate it live and unscripted!

I explained my concerns and asked the interrupter if they would be ok acting as a guinea pig. They were happy to. I asked the group how they thought I could use BUILD to describe the behaviour. Then we had a conversation about whether each statement was a fact or a judgement.

We tried: "Can you please stop interrupting me." We agreed this was an order. It might quiet the interruption short term, but it would leave them angry. No one likes being ordered about.

"Could I please finish my presentation first before we take questions?" This is less judgemental. But because it's a question, it opens a dialogue too soon. It leaves the other person in charge of the conversation.

"You've interrupted me while I'm speaking." This is more neutral, but "interrupting" suggests some negative motivation. As we get more skilled at describing behaviours, we build a subtle understanding of language that seems factual at first but is actually judgemental.

"You are being aggressive." We know this is a red flag. With 'you are', the alarm bells should start ringing. Because that's when you know a judgement is coming: rude, insensitive, mean. These are judgements that describe personality traits, not behaviours. Judgements put the other person on the defensive. They are much more likely to disagree, and so you are much more likely to argue.

If you must bring up personality traits, they belong here in the Impact stage of BUILD. "When you said that, it felt mean to me." Remember, your aim is not to be right. It's to give the other person room to learn and change.

We settled on, "You spoke while I was talking." This is a factual observation. It sets out the situation accurately. They have to agree this is true.

Time to describe the impact.

We agreed on, "People are losing track and we are all concerned I won't get to the end of my presentation or that we will overrun."

BUILD is beautifully simple. All you need to do is say two things and ask two questions.

The two things you say:

- Describe the behaviour.
- Describe the impact.

That's what we did as a group. We described the behaviour (you spoke while I was talking) and then the impact (people are losing track and we are all concerned I won't get to the end of my presentation or that we will overrun).

If you would like to practise this, you might try what my workshop group did. Think about your Chosen Conversation and write down a few options for how you could describe the behaviour. Then examine each and decide which ones include a little judgement, and which are plain old facts.

Now you ask two questions:

- What's happening here?
- What could you / we do differently?

In my workshop example, I asked them, "What was happening there?"

They explained that they had a couple of key points they wanted to make and were worried there wouldn't be time at the end for questions.

After I listened to their concerns, we moved to the last stage of BUILD. I asked them, "What could we do differently?" I realised that I hadn't made it clear that I would present for fifteen minutes and there would be fifteen minutes at the end for discussion. We agreed some updated timings and moved on.

Let's take a closer look at those two questions and how you can use them to create kinder conversations.

10

LISTEN UP

We've talked about how to choose kind and non-judgemental words for the conversations you need to have. But the last two steps of BUILD are about listening. Listening is key to the Kinder Feedback Method. The more we practise listening, the better we get at it. And the better we get at listening, the easier it is to step into other people's shoes.

Listening seems like an easy step. You just sit there and say nothing. But effective listening takes focus and practice.

I'm sorry to break the news, but most of us don't listen nearly as much as we think we do! To ease the blow, let's look at a couple of studies about family doctors.

A report found that family doctors overestimated the time they spend listening by... what do you think? Whatever you guess, I promise it's even more than that.

They overestimated not by 100% or 200% or even 300%, but by a whopping 700%. The doctors thought they'd been listening for seven minutes, but in fact it had only been one minute.

Another study observed doctors listening to patients explain their symptoms and worries.[1] This is the part of the appointment that lets the doctor know what the problem is, so they can start diagnosis. These doctors understood that, and they'd received dedicated training in listening. Yet they still only waited eleven seconds before interrupting.

If these highly skilled and trained people can get it so wrong, it's not so surprising that we can too.

We all know how it feels when someone doesn't listen. Maybe you got excited about a promotion, but when you told your partner they said off-handedly, "That's great." Or perhaps you had an important personal breakthrough that you wanted to share with your best friend, but they couldn't put their smartphone down long enough to give you their full attention.

Sometimes it even feels like the other person is judging us, like when you tell your dad about your kid getting into university and he responds with, "The kid down the road just got into Oxford. Let me tell you all about it…"

It doesn't feel good, does it? And it can have a big impact. When you are giving feedback to someone about something that's so important to you, would you like them to be anxious, confused and self-absorbed? Or would you prefer them to be calm, clear and self-aware?

A study showed that distracted listeners who look at their smartphone or constantly interrupt leave the speaker feeling more anxious, less self-aware, and not so clear about their own attitudes to the topic at hand.[2]

On the flip side, when someone truly listens to us it's delightful. Can you remember a time when you shared something important and the other person genuinely listened? Think about how it felt to have their full attention. Maybe you told your best friend about an idea for your next creative project and they lit up and told you, "That sounds wonderful!" Or maybe you shared a concern with a colleague, who nodded and said thoughtfully, "I can really see why that worries you. Shall we talk about possible solutions?"

When you listen well, you help the speaker feel relaxed enough to share deeper thoughts and discover new insights about themselves.

Listening is a powerful tool for kinder conversations. And to help us, we can use the listening ladder. The listening ladder shows that there are four levels of listening.

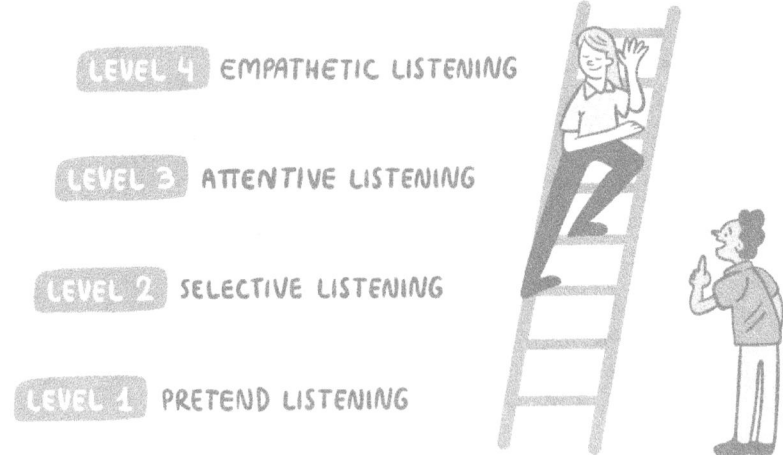

Let's walk up the ladder.

Starting at level 1, we have pretend listening. We're not concentrating. We're definitely not focused on the speaker. We're thinking about that email we have to write later, or that we forgot to add rice vinegar to the shopping list. We might reply with the occasional "ummm" or a "stock safe reply." Really? That's great! Yeah. Then what? And the like. We're not listening – and they know it.

Then at level 2 we've got selective listening. You experience this every day, and you probably do it every day too. We take in just enough information to confirm our biases or judgements. If you catch yourself thinking, "I knew they were going to say that," you're probably selectively listening. Or you hear just enough to find a way to cut in with your own point of view. "Oh, you're planning a holiday? We've just been on holiday – it was great – let me tell you all about it."

At level two you're still not really listening – and they still know it.

At level 3 we have attentive listening. Now we're getting somewhere. We're genuinely listening to what they're saying. We're interested. We ask questions like, "Can you tell me more about that?" And they're good questions, the kind that are helpful to the speaker rather than just there to satisfy our curiosity. At level 3 we don't judge, evaluate, or leap to conclusions. We take off those sticky notes of judgement. We're truly listening now – and the other person knows it. But we're still limited to the words we're hearing.

Level 4, empathetic listening, is the Olympic gold standard of listening. At level 4 we don't just listen to the words, we notice what else is going on. We hear their tone of voice and pick up on their body language. We respond in kind so they know we feel empathy for their situation.

This kind of empathetic listening is even more vital when it comes to giving kinder feedback. Studies show that when speakers feel listeners are being empathetic, attentive and non-judgemental, they relax more. They share their inner thoughts without worrying about what the listener thinks of them. This is much more conducive to a productive conversation.

When you listen well, the speaker has more 'attitude complexity'. That means they're more likely to see both sides of the situation. That's right. Just by listening to them, hearing them, and giving them the time they need to express their views, you're helping them create a more balanced view.

That means they're more likely to acknowledge a need and desire to change their behaviour.

Now you may feel there are some people out there with no self-awareness. But being properly listened to makes people more aware of their weaknesses, as well as their strengths. Listening to someone helps them become more self-aware.

June was irritated with her nephew. Whenever he came to stay, he'd leave crisp packets and chocolate wrappers on the floor instead of putting them in the bin. When June tried to raise it, he told her to "chill." That felt dismissive.

So June used BUILD. "You said I should chill." He acknowledged that he had. They agreed. June explained the impact. "When you told me to chill, it made me feel that you don't respect my home. What's happening here?"

"What's happening here?" is a good lead-in to listening. We'll talk more about that in a moment.

"I'm just so tired from my classes," June's nephew told her. "When I come to stay, it's good to let go and relax a bit. But I can see how that might look messy."

They were able to move to the next stage – what could you do differently? He suggested putting a wastepaper bin in the guest bedroom so he didn't have to go far to dispose of rubbish. They both enjoyed his visits more.

Empathetic listening encourages people to identify resources that might help them and opportunities to change within themselves. That way, when you get to the next step of BUILD (ask what we might do differently) they're more likely to find positive solutions.

If you find it hard to listen sometimes, that's ok. It's natural. Listening well takes time and effort. You might be worried about what you'll hear. You might even feel like listening is giving up power (when you're talking, it feels like you're in control). But it's a skill you can learn and get better at.

Gandhi once said, "Be the change you want to see in the world." Neuroscience has caught Gandhi up and proved him right. Emotions are contagious. We've all felt down because someone around us is in a black mood, or been lifted by infectious laughter. But did you know behaviours are contagious too?[3] When you genuinely listen to someone, they're more likely to listen to you. They're more likely to hear the issue you need them to hear, acknowledge it, and take action.

Listening starts with asking the right question. In the Kinder Feedback Method, we often start with, "What was happening there?" It's a clean question, simple and with no judgement.

If you ask, "What was going on?" or "What is happening with you?" you've got a bit of judgement sneaking in there. These questions are a little bit pointy-fingered.

And whatever you do, don't ask *why*. "Why did you do that?" *Why* suggests that they owe you an explanation. And out will come all the justifications and reasons. "Why?" is a really unhelpful question.

You want to let the other person know that you genuinely want to hear their point of view. You're not demanding an explanation, just listening.

Another variation you can use is, "I'd love to hear your perspective." Isn't that gentle? It lets them know that you value what they have to say.

Once they start talking, give them a good level 4 listening to. Don't get into a discussion. Your job is not to discuss the whys and wherefores of their view. Just listen.

Don't agree or disagree. Just listen.

Don't say yes or no. Just listen.

When they're done talking – and do let them finish talking before you speak – acknowledge that they've been heard. A simple, "Ok, I hear you" works great.

Think again of your Chosen Conversation. In your mind, rehearse saying, "What was happening there?" or "I'd love to hear your perspective," and then just listening. Imagine hearing genuine, open reasons and thoughts, instead of pushback and cross words.

Imagine how much that would improve this situation.

11

WHAT MIGHT YOU DO DIFFERENTLY?

Asking someone else to change their behaviour feels challenging. You might feel like it's not possible to speak up without messing up and making the situation worse. You're expecting pushback. Maybe you're concerned about trying to force them to do what's right for you.

Asking "what might you do differently?" makes it much easier to speak up.

This part of BUILD is coaching – it encourages the hearer to find their own solutions, rather than you telling them yours. "What might you do differently?" is collaborative rather than confrontational. It opens the way for a conversation.

Javier's sister was grinding his gears. She had a habit of dropping off her kids for him to look after without asking him first. Like many of us now, Javier has started to work from home so his sister knows he'll be there and he really loves them. But he's feeling like she's starting to take advantage of him. Javier used BUILD to state her behaviour without judgement. "You dropped the kids off yesterday without asking if I was ok with it, and checking if I was home." They could agree on that. Javier stepped into her shoes. Maybe she had an urgent situation going on. Or maybe she was excited for him to spend time with his niece and nephew.

What about the impact? "I love having them, but I'm starting to feel a bit put upon, and concerned that if I had not been available you might not have had time to make other arrangements, and the kids might have been disappointed. What was happening there?"

His sister admitted that she got so busy at work that she sometimes forgot to call and ask in advance. Javier asked, "What might you do differently?" His sister told him that in future she would set up a phone reminder so she'd remember to reach out to him at least 24 hours in advance.

Javier asked, "What might you do differently?" But you can phrase the question in different ways, if that suits the situation better. Choose the way that feels most comfortable for you. You can ask, "What could we do differently so this works for all of us?" or "What could we do together to resolve this?"

These options are even more collaborative.

Of course, we're all human, and no one likes to feel criticised. So don't be surprised if sometimes when you ask, "What could we do differently?" the response you get is something the other person would like you to do. If that happens, simply acknowledge it with, "Ok, I hear you," and then ask, "and what could you do?"

When you ask this question, you're giving the other person the chance to come up with their own ideas. This is better for everyone. Motivation is an intrinsic force. We have to want something internally to really go for it. People are much more likely to act on their own ideas. Asking, "What might we do differently?" lets them come up with an idea they're motivated to act on.

Have you ever jumped in to fill an awkward silence with whatever comes to your mind? I think we all have. After you ask this question, it might be tempting to start adding your own suggestions, but resist. Don't nudge them. Give them the space to come up with their own answer, while you practise your level 4 listening skills.

When you let the other person come up with their own ideas, often they'll come up with something we didn't expect but that works for them.

I walked into the office kitchen to find a co-worker had left a mess. (It really seems to happen everywhere for me!) I used BUILD to give kinder feedback: "Your lunch stuff was left in the sink, Simon. I had to wash it up before I could do mine. What was happening?"

Simon told me he'd simply forgotten as he was eating his pasta at his desk and started replying to an urgent email.

So, I asked, "Simon, what might you do differently?"

What do you suppose he said? I know I was expecting him to talk about washing up sooner, leaving the sink clear for other staff members. But instead, he said, "You know, I never have the time to wash up. Maybe I'll bring sandwiches from now on, then I don't have to bother."

Simon got an easier lunch time with no washing up, and I got a clean sink so I could do my dishes and prep my own lunch. The solution worked for everybody.

When asking the question, don't try to make a suggestion or push them into your desired outcome. No matter how well intentioned, this is still a telling-off – you're telling them what you think they should do. Just ask and then listen.

In the next chapter we're going to walk through the BUILD steps for your Chosen Conversation. But for now, can you imagine asking this question? It might seem difficult at first, but think about the outcomes: a gentler conversation, and a solution they're motivated to implement.

12

PUTTING IT INTO ACTION

Take a moment now to think about your Chosen Conversation. We've talked a bit in each chapter about how you might use BUILD in this situation. Now let's walk through it together.

DESCRIBE THE **BEHAVIOUR**

UNDERSTAND THEIR CONTEXT

DESCRIBE THE **IMPACT**

LISTEN TO THEM

ASK WHAT MIGHT YOU/WE **DO DIFFERENTLY?**

Start with B – the behaviour. How would you describe their behaviour factually and without judgement? Try to state it in a way that most people would agree with.

State calmly what they did or said: "You told me you are too busy to return my call." "You pointed out my mistake in front of the team."

But don't bring up their attitude or personality traits: "You don't return my calls because you don't care." "You pointed out my mistake because you wanted me to feel embarrassed." This is also not the time to talk about how you feel – that belongs in the impact step. All you need to do right now is answer the question, "What did they say or do?" as objectively as you can.

Pause for a moment with U – understand. Step into their shoes, with as much generosity as you can manage. What might be going on in their life to cause this behaviour? Maybe their boss has been intolerable lately. Or they've received some bad news. Or they've had the kind of day when the bus was late, they spilled coffee on their shoes, and their lunch exploded in the microwave.

You don't have to be right. You probably won't be right. You most likely won't ever know, and that's ok. Stepping into their shoes punctures a small hole in your bubble of self-righteous indignation. No judgement here. It's normal to get a bit self-righteous when someone's behaviour irritates or upsets us. But activating your empathy will subtly change your tone of voice, making you less argumentative, and giving them room to reflect and grow. Remember the U is unsaid. It is just quiet thinking.

Now move onto the I – impact. How would you describe their impact on you, the family, the team, someone else, the project or the world? You can describe your feelings in this step. How did you feel? And what was the knock-on effect of that? "When you didn't return my call, I was concerned that we wouldn't have time to arrange the outing we talked about." Or "When you mentioned my mistake at the meeting it felt like I was being singled out in front of the team."

State it calmly and remember not to assume intent. Say, "When you used that tone it made me feel that you don't take my experience seriously," rather than, "You never take me seriously because you think I'm under-qualified."

Then it's time to listen. Listening turns what could have been a telling-off into a conversation. It's key to talking it out without falling out – because you give them space to share their side.

What's the best or most comfortable way for you to ask for their point of view? Find words that are open and inviting. "What was happening? I'd like to hear your perspective." Steer clear of judgemental questions like, "Why did you do that?" or "What were you thinking?" Remember, you're not questioning their motives. This is not an interrogation. You are genuinely interested in their views and experience.

Listen. Just listen. Don't agree or disagree. Don't say yes or no. Don't argue about their view. Just listen. And when they're finished speaking, simply say, "Ok, I hear you." Now they feel heard, and not like they've been told off. It's an equal conversation.

It's time to move on to the final step – asking what we could do differently.

I was working with a mediator at a university that chose BUILD as its universal approach to feedback and bystander intervention. They described the D step in BUILD as restorative justice. You've been heard. They've been heard. Now here's a chance for change.

Rehearse asking them, "What might you do differently?" Or you could go with, "What could we do differently so this works for both of us?"

Now give it a go, using the worksheet on the next page.

YOUR CHOSEN CONVERSATION

Use this template to work out how you will phrase your BUILD feedback

	YOUR SITUATION	ON FURTHER REFLECTION
B BEHAVIOUR		
U UNDERSTAND		
I IMPACT		
L LISTEN		
D DO DIFFERENTLY		

PART III

BUILD IN ACTION

13

ALL THE BENEFITS OF BUILD

So now you've explored BUILD, what do you like about it?

Maybe it's the B. Describing behaviours in a non-judgemental way takes the heat out of the situation. It de-escalates things. By starting with agreement, you're already heading down a path that's more likely to reach a resolution.

Perhaps you like the U? Stepping into their shoes with empathy and trying to understand the pressures on them is a good way to open yourself up to a helpful dialogue. Your empathy softens your tone of voice, making your feedback easier to hear.

Or you might like the I. Letting them know the impact they had on you means you can state what feels true for you, and they can reflect and learn. It's giving the gift of insight, and the opportunity to change. Giving feedback is an act of kindness.

Maybe L is your favourite step. When you ask for their view and then listen, they do most of the speaking. Now it's a genuine conversation. Your curious listening opens up their self-awareness.

Or, like the university mediator, your favourite step might be the D. You appreciate the focus on resolution and what everyone could do differently. Things can work better in the future, can't they?

My favourite step is, truthfully, all of them. I like BUILD because it's quick and structured. In the heat of the moment this simplicity is vital. You know where you're headed and there's light at the end of the tunnel. That's the beauty of BUILD feedback.

BUILD FOR SELF-REFLECTION

So far we've focused on using the BUILD approach as part of giving kinder feedback to others. But there's one other person in your relationships who might also find it helpful. And that's you.

Self-reflection helps us think about things that worked and how we can learn from that. And it helps us think about things that didn't work so we can reflect on how to make things better next time.

When something doesn't work out the way you'd like, you can use BUILD to give yourself feedback.

Think about your chosen conversation and your relationship with the other person. Remember a time when things didn't go well, perhaps a time they did the thing you need to give feedback on. Or maybe a time when you tried to give feedback and it wasn't well received.

[B] WHAT DID I DO?
[U] SOME EMPATHY FOR MYSELF?
[I] WHAT WAS THE IMPACT?
[L] WHAT WAS HAPPENING FOR ME?
[D] WHAT MIGHT I DO DIFFERENTLY?

How did you behave? What did you say or do, and what tone of voice did you use? Can you describe the impact you might have had on them? You can look forward with this question too – what impact would you like to have? What would you like the outcome to be? Perhaps if you think about what outcome they might like too, you can find some common ground.

What story might they have made up in their mind about you and the relationship?

Now you can ask yourself, "So what was happening there for me?" and listen to yourself carefully. You're not trying to justify your actions. Just exploring your motivations, actions and reactions. Let yourself be curious and see what comes up.

Knowing what you know now, what might you do differently next time?

14

TALK TO THE HAND

BUILD feedback works for most of us, most of the time. But sometimes people don't want to receive feedback. Or, like with Sally's experience with the angry doctor, it takes time for the feedback to sink in and for them to reflect.

But what should you do if you give feedback and they tell you, "Well, I'm not going to change anything?"

If this is the first time you've spoken about this, they might just need time to think about it. They might come around. Give them time. You might find that, like Sally, in an hour or a day or a week, that person will seek you out and thank you.

But if they truly don't want to hear your feedback, you can be at peace with that too. You can simply say, "Ok, I just thought you might like to know," and walk away.

Remember, your intention is not to change the other person. You've still offered them the gift of self-awareness. Just as with any other gift, once it's in their hands, they can do with it what they will, including ignoring it.

What if they still don't change? What can you do when you've given feedback to someone several times about an issue, but they haven't changed their behaviour?

Guess what? You can use BUILD to feedback about their lack of action.

Behaviour: "I have given you feedback about this on several occasions, including when we spoke yesterday, and your behaviour hasn't changed."

Understand: This behaviour is clearly very deep rooted for them, perhaps caused by some harm or trauma they suffered earlier in their life. I imagine that's really difficult.

Impact: "I'm concerned that you've not understood the impact this is having on…"

Listen: "Is there anything else you'd like to talk to me about around this?"

What can we **do differently**? "Ok, I hear you. Is there anything you'd like to try to do differently?" And perhaps, "I wonder from my perspective if you could try to do this instead. How might you go about doing this?"

Changing behaviour can be hard, but most people, most of the time, want to have a positive impact on the people around them. Sometimes, you may not be the right person to give the feedback, or they're not ready to hear it. If it's a work situation you might need to move to more formal mediation, performance management, or a disciplinary process.

By starting with BUILD, you're giving the situation the best chance for a resolution. You're finding a resolution sooner, so molehills don't get turned into mountains. And you're helping your friend, family member or colleague to stop their harmful behaviour.

Some people don't want to hear.

Sometimes when I teach the Kinder Feedback Method, people tell me that not everyone wants feedback. Not everyone is willing to hear it. They're not interested in changing! So why bother trying?

I get what they mean but let me ask you this. Has it ever been you – honestly – that perhaps caused someone else's bad day through your behaviour?

The chances are it has. Not because you're a bad person, but because we all have an impact on the people around us every time we interact. And sometimes that impact is negative. Wouldn't you rather know so you can do something about it instead of causing harm and not having a clue that you did?

Of course you would. If you don't know, you can't change. It might be hard to hear, but I'm willing to bet you wouldn't want to have harmed someone, not know, and not have the chance to apologise, make amends and change.

Most of us would rather know there's a problem. I know speaking up is scary. But don't let your projection of how they might react turn into a reason to say nothing.

WHEN AND WHERE?

I'm often asked, when is the right time to give feedback? Should you do it right then, when the behaviour has just happened? Or is it better to wait?

Every situation is different so there are no hard and fast rules. But one piece of advice I would give is to be timely, to speak up as soon as possible.

Say you're managing a small team. If your team member says something concerning during a meeting with the whole team, it might be best to wait and have a word in private after the meeting. That way, you avoid the team member feeling embarrassed.

But it's important to pick up some things at the time so everyone can learn. Hurtful behaviour, errors in agreed process, or actions that might harm safety or wellbeing shouldn't be left hanging. When you pick them up immediately, you model good behaviour for the whole team. You let them know that this is not the kind of thing we get away with around here.

I was having lunch in a busy hospital restaurant in East London when a young person with a stethoscope walked in with three colleagues. She was clearly oblivious to where she was, ranting to her colleagues in language that would make anyone's ears turn blue. I could see that patients, caregivers and other staff alike were shocked, embarrassed and offended. I stood up and stated the behaviour and impact without judgement. "People can hear what you are saying. I'm offended and I imagine others are too." She looked around, put her hand to her mouth, said, "I'm so sorry," and sat down.

In situations where feedback cannot wait, BUILD is the kindest way to offer it. You don't have to schedule a meeting. You don't have to book a room. You just pick the right time and start building solutions.

DO WE ALWAYS HAVE TO SAY SOMETHING?

Take a look at this helpful piece of graffiti. We know that our perspective is only one view of the situation. So do we always have to speak up?

If someone is at risk of harm, then yes, of course we do. Remember, if we say nothing, nothing changes.

But there are some situations where giving feedback isn't the best course of action.

If someone makes a one-off comment or mistake that doesn't have a significant impact, you might choose to have a little empathy, understand, forgive and move on. You always have the option to practise the Kinder Feedback Method if it becomes an ongoing issue. But you don't always have to jump right in.

There are also situations where giving feedback might not feel safe. If you feel that the other person means you harm, of course you don't have to stop and give them feedback. If someone is about to mug you, I don't suggest you stop and tell them, "You are about to mug me, which means I will not have my wallet." Get out of there and call the police. Likewise, if you can tell someone is spoiling for a fight, you don't have to attend that fight.

If a person or situation is toxic and you need to – and can – walk away, give yourself permission to do that.

The Kinder Feedback Method is for situations where you hope to see a change and create a more positive relationship.

FIND A BUILD BUDDY

Giving BUILD feedback is a new skill, and just like any other skill, you'll get better with practice. It's just like riding a bike. You'll fall off and graze your knees occasionally, but you'll keep growing in confidence.

So why not find yourself a BUILD buddy to practise with? This doesn't have to be super serious – you can have some fun with it. My BUILD buddy was one of my kids when they were younger.

Behaviour: "I just made a joke and you didn't laugh."

Impact: "It makes me think you don't think I'm hilarious."

Listen: "What's happening here?"

"Well, to be honest, these dad jokes have never been funny – I'm just humouring you."

Do differently: "What might we do differently?"

"I'll get you a joke book for Christmas."

When you practise BUILD, it helps you get the structure "into the muscle." You'll find it easier to follow the five steps.

You'll get better at describing behaviour non-judgementally. You can even practise with your buddy before the feedback about your Chosen Conversation. Practise together so you can become skilled and confident in giving kinder feedback whenever you need to.

15

BUILD FOR EVERY SITUATION

You can apply BUILD to so many situations. Let's look at some of those in more detail and see if these help you to get even clearer about your own Chosen Conversation.

BUILD FOR BYSTANDER INTERVENTION

People sometimes ask me if it's ok to use BUILD to describe what you imagine the impact might be on another person even if that person isn't present. Or if you can use BUILD in a situation that doesn't directly impact you.

The answer is yes. This came up for me a little while ago.

I was doing some Kinder Culture consulting with a tech company, and we'd broken for lunch. I overheard a conversation in which three people were talking about another colleague in a way I found disrespectful. I didn't feel comfortable letting that slide so I eased my way into their space. I listened for a moment to be sure I hadn't misunderstood the situation.

I gently interrupted them. "You're talking about Barbara when she isn't in the room. I imagine she might be upset if she heard what you were saying. What's happening here?"

You might be wondering if I was nervous about speaking up. I was. It's not easy to walk up to a group of near strangers and give them feedback about their behaviour. We'll touch later on how to get past the fear of giving feedback.

Speaking up was the right thing for me to do, and it will be for you too. But the 'bystander effect' shows that, counter-intuitively, the more people who witness an event, the less likely it is someone will speak up about it. And studies show witnesses to rudeness are 50% less likely to offer help to anyone around them.[1]

So it takes effort. You may want to stay alert to situations where you might be a bystander, but you can still make a difference by speaking up. The more you practise BUILD, the more you'll see opportunities to use it to help people like Barbara who aren't there to defend themselves. Or people who are there, but who need a friendly person to step in and help them.

BUILD AT HOME

Many of my workshop participants go on to use BUILD at home and with their families. It's a gentle tool that helps you have important conversations with the people you live with.

Meilin was feeling cross at her roommate, Alexis, because she never cleaned the bathroom when it was her turn. Meilin tended to avoid rather than attack so she hadn't talked to Alexis. But she had done a lot of muttering under her breath, and sometimes cleaning the bathroom herself with bad grace.

With BUILD she was able to state her case calmly. "You didn't clean the bathroom when it was your turn." She could talk about her feelings (the impact) without accusing: "It makes me feel like you don't take our chore schedule seriously, and I end up doing more."

Alexis admitted she hated cleaning the bathroom but acknowledged it wasn't fair to Meilin. Alexis suggested an unexpected solution that worked for both of them: if Meilin cleaned the bathroom, Alexis would take over Meilin's most hated chore of taking out the rubbish and recycling. The house looked better and more importantly, their relationship was more positive.

BUILD FOR A KINDER WORKPLACE

I've asked several leaders and managers the question, "Is performance management bullying?"

Their immediate response is always, "No, it isn't. It's helping someone meet the standards expected in their role." Then I'll see the cogs turn as they think it over before saying, "Performance management isn't bullying if it's done right."

BUILD helps you have important work conversations "right."

When it comes to performance management, people love better feedback. A study by Gallup[2] found that setting goals together and giving feedback about how people are doing in meeting those goals is one of the top things managers can do to improve employee engagement.

John had a colleague, Nia, whom he'd tasked with delivering the figures for their monthly reports. But Nia was almost always late delivering them. John could feel his frustration rising until he was afraid he might explode with an attack: Why can't you just do your job!

So John took his new BUILD skills and tried a non-judgemental approach. "You delivered the figures at the last minute." They could both agree on that. John thought about what might be going on – maybe Nia was busy and had too much on her plate. He shared the impact: "It means I have to stay late and I'm afraid I won't be able to deliver the report on time, or to the highest standards. What's happening here?"

Nia explained that her line manager tended to throw a lot of work at her, and the figures got pushed to the bottom of the pile. John asked, "So what could we do differently?" Nia agreed to talk to her line manager about her workload.

We've talked about tweaking the D step of BUILD from, "What could you do differently?" to, "What could we do differently?" This is particularly effective at work. It gives the other party the chance to speak up for the support they need.

BUILD FOR SPEAKING UP ABOUT SAFETY

I boarded a short flight from London to Edinburgh a few years ago. The captain introduced himself over the tannoy as Captain Martin Bromily. I recognised his name at once. In 2005, Martin's wife Elaine died during a routine operation. The doctors told Martin, "We're sorry, but these things happen."

But as a pilot, Martin knew that in aviation it's never 'just one of those things'. There's always an independent investigation. So, Martin pushed until he got a proper investigation into his wife's death. They found that during the operation, Elaine's airway collapsed and the surgical team took twenty-five minutes trying to intubate her. They thought it had taken them less than ten.

The nurses in the room saw clear signs that Elaine was struggling. They were surprised the doctors didn't attempt to gain access to the trachea, but didn't know how to broach the subject. One nurse took matters into her own hands and presented the doctors with a tracheostomy set, but they didn't acknowledge her. Another nurse phoned the ICU and told them to prepare a bed. When she told the doctors, they looked at her as if she was overreacting.

That investigation taught us so much about human factors. I think it also shows the danger of not feeling confident or knowing how to speak up about a safety issue.[3]

At the end of the flight, I thanked Martin, on behalf of us all, for his courage in helping to build cultures where it no longer takes courage to speak up. (A surreptitious ABC.)

BUILD TO SUPPORT STAFF WELLBEING

Richard was walking along the corridor at work when he noticed the team in his colleague Monica's office were hunched over their computers as they worked. Worried about their postures, Richard walked in and told Monica, "Your team can't work sitting like that! You need to take better care of how they sit."

Do you think that got a positive response? If you guess no, you're right. Monica told him, "I'm far too busy for this," and carried on with her work.

So Richard went chuntering along the corridor, muttering to himself about how he'd only been trying to help, didn't she care about her team's safety, and so on. But Richard knew BUILD and realised this was an ideal time to use it. He tried stepping into her shoes – perhaps she had an urgent deadline.

He went back to Monica's office and stated the behaviour. "I mentioned that your team's posture seemed to be unsafe, and you said you were too busy for it."

The impact? "I'm concerned about your team's physical health. I'm also worried that because you did not respond to my suggestions, they might get the impression that you don't care. What was happening there?"

Monica told him that she agrees it's important but had an urgent deadline in an hour and didn't have time to stop and talk about it then. "Why don't you come back this afternoon and we can have a proper chat?"

BUILD gives you a way to offer fearlessly gentle feedback even in awkward situations.

BUILD FOR MEDIATION

Lisa is an NHS manager. She was struggling with two doctors at war. Doctor Conway would fill out the notes in the way they had always done it, and Doctor Patel would tell him they were wrong. Doctor Patel asked a patient some questions, and Doctor Conway interrupted them – in front of the patient.

Lisa was at her wits' end. She'd tried everything, including coaching and mediation. She felt like she was stuck between an argumentative rock and a stubborn hard place.

But then Lisa learned about BUILD and the results were amazing. She talked the doctors through BUILD and they took turns to give each other feedback and hear each other's side of the story. Doctor Patel told Doctor Conway, "You interrupted me while I was talking with a patient. I was concerned this might undermine the patient's confidence in me. What was happening there?"

Doctor Conway explained that they were eager to cover all bases and wanted to make sure Doctor Patel didn't miss a question.

Using BUILD they both began to understand the impact their behaviour was having on each other and the wider team. They changed their practice as a result. The whole team is now much happier, and the doctors have a strong working relationship.

BUILD turned the fraught situation into a positive outcome.

BUILD is excellent in other mediation situations too. One of my friends, Luke, tried it with his kids.

"They couldn't agree on what to watch for family film night. Using BUILD they were able to talk calmly about it. Inès said that Jules rejected every suggestion she made about what to watch. It made her feel that her wants didn't matter. Jules admitted he felt tired after a hard week at school and wanted to relax with a film he loved. They agreed on one they could both enjoy!"

BUILD TO SPEAK UP AGAINST BULLYING

One of the reasons I do this work is because I was once involved in a bullying situation at work. It started with lots of nit picking. That escalated into questioning quality and ability. Then came isolation and exclusion. The outcome? Anxiety, a severe loss of confidence, and a prescription for beta blockers.

Recent studies show there's too much of this behaviour in our world and in our workplaces.

So what is bullying? Agreed definitions say it's a repeated action, not just one-off rudeness. It's unwelcome. Whether it was meant or not doesn't matter – if it meets the definition, it's still bullying.

Bullying shows up in four main ways:

- Gossip, which can be made even worse by social exclusion or scapegoating.
- Insults, criticism, personal comments or humiliation. This can be the most obvious form of

bullying, but it can be subtle too. It's sometimes disguised as banter.
- Intimidation or misuse of power. I see this a lot in my work with organisations. In our studies we find people are as likely to be bullied by a colleague as by a manager.
- And of course, there's work-related harassment. This includes withholding information, having responsibilities taken away without consultation, and work overload.

My first experience of bullying was my dad's boss. Whenever dad wrote a report, he'd take dad's name off and replace it with his. I saw first-hand the debilitating impact this had on my dad, and how his lowered self-esteem and frustration followed him home.

With bullying, everyone loses. Not only the target of bullying, but their team and organisation, their family and even their friends. Bullying harms productivity, it harms quality, and it harms people. 50% of people who experience bullying suffer from depression, 60% from heart palpitations and insomnia, and 75% from memory problems, loss of concentration and overwhelming anxiety.[4]

And over 80% suffer from the "anticipation of the next negative event," otherwise known as "walking on eggshells."

Right now, I can hear some of you saying, "Come on, Tim. I can see how BUILD is great for speaking up about a range of behaviours, but surely bullying is a whole different wheelhouse?" BUILD still works though. Let's talk about that.

Bullying can be hard to define. In our age of social media, click-bait and five-second soundbites, it's easy to reduce things to a broad generalisation of "bullying." But when we look under the hood, we find out people's experiences can be subtle. In our surveys, around 25% of people say they've been bullied at work in the last six months. But when we ask how often they've experienced the poor behaviour, around one-third of those people say once or twice.

Once or twice isn't typically bullying. If we want to get beyond bullying and speak up about it safely, we need to know if "bullying" is the right word. We can use the B of BUILD to factually describe the specific behaviours. Then we can use the following guide to figure out if it's bullying:

This poster has been used to great effect in schools. We've also built it into our Respectful Resolution pathway, which organisations use to reduce and resolve issues with bullying and other poor behaviour in the workplace, to great effect.

We said earlier that it's still bullying even if it's unintentional. Let's revisit that. The fact is, if you don't tell them, they might not know. In just and fair cultures, if someone does something we don't like, we tell them, using BUILD, so they have a chance to learn, grow and change.

One of our workshop participants, Haruto, admitted he'd been feeling bullied by a colleague. He'd tried to talk it out without falling out but found himself saying, "You're a bully!" That put the other person on the defensive.

If someone's feeling victimised, they often respond with, "You're bullying me," or, "You're a bully." Even if the other person's actions meet the definition of bullying, this still puts them on edge. Telling someone they're a bully raises the emotional temperature and they're likely to disagree.

Using BUILD, Haruto was able to state calmly, "You've called me out in front of the team four times now." That's the behaviour. Because we can bring our feelings into the impact stage if we need to, Haruto said, "It felt like a direct criticism, it was embarrassing and it feels a little bit like bullying to me." Then listen: "What's happening here? I'd like your perspective."

Haruto's colleague admitted that he was feeling out of his depth in his new role and felt that Haruto's ideas undermined his own. With BUILD they were able to reach an understanding – that he would raise issues with Haruto in private if he needed to, and also seek the support he needed.

Remember, your aim in giving feedback is not to be right. Being right won't make things better, though you might feel vindicated. And you're not trying to "make them see" that they're a bully. You're looking to have a kinder conversation about the situation so you can find a resolution.

The ABCs of Appreciation are useful here, too. Counter-intuitively, appreciation can also reduce poor behaviour. One study found that aggressive behaviour is often caused by lack of confidence. Because praise boosts confidence, it can help to reduce aggressive behaviour.

Of course, you don't thank the person for being horrible! But people aren't angels or devils. We are just fallible humans. So, speak up with BUILD about what isn't working.

Then notice what they do that is worthy of praise and appreciate that. You'll see your relationship with them change. You'll see their behaviours change. So many relationships can be improved by appreciation.

And BUILD gives you the structure you need to start even difficult-seeming conversations in all kinds of situations. You'll find it works in almost any situation, whether that's about behaviour, performance, safety, bullying, or more entrenched relationship issues.

Go back to the worksheet at the end of the previous chapter and consider your Chosen Conversation. How might your deeper understanding of kinder feedback change the words you choose?

16

SPEAKING UP ABOUT RACISM

As I was editing the final draft of this book, I was asked by NHS England to give a presentation on using BUILD to speak up as a by-stander to racism. I'm so grateful for the input of friends, colleagues and clients into this section, especially those who have experienced racism firsthand and so bravely shared their experiences so others can benefit.

Throughout this book names have been changed to protect confidentiality. I presented online to 750 NHS colleagues passionate about improving equality, diversity and inclusion. Their positive feedback persuaded me to include the contents of the presentation here.

Racism has caused and continues to cause deep and significant harm to individuals and communities. When we see racism, we want to call it out. But it feels hard. You might be anxious that you will be victimised. It might cause an argument, or damage an important work relationship, or even damage your career.

Maybe you're afraid of being branded a troublemaker, being isolated or ostracised, maybe accused of being too emotional. You may worry all of this will happen and still nothing will actually change.

And we need to change things.

We often think about racism as overt racist or discriminatory acts, things like using racist words or making sweeping or hurtful generalisations. We imagine someone being intentionally and directly excluded because of the colour of their skin, their religious beliefs, or the country their grandparents grew up in.

The impact of these can be devastating. But often racism takes the shape of less overt, but no less harmful, micro-aggressions such as being asked, "Where are you from originally?" Or being mistaken for the other Asian person on your floor at work. Or insensitive banter (often passed off as a 'joke') about your food, beliefs, or other aspects of your culture. These subtle acts of exclusion can have a significant impact. They might not be meant as racism, but just because harm isn't intended that doesn't mean it isn't caused.

Racism affects people at work, such as not being offered a role you're fully qualified for, being overlooked for a promotion you're ready for, or not being given access to training that other members of the team have benefitted from.

Studies from past decades showed that when identical CVs were submitted with an English sounding name and then with an Indian one, the English name was more likely to be shortlisted.[1]

You'd hope by now we'd be past this kind of discriminatory treatment. But sadly, we are not. In the wonderfully multicultural NHS a White person is still 1.6 times more likely to be offered a role when shortlisted than someone from a Black, Asian or minority ethnic (BAME) background. This person has been shortlisted for the same role, so they're clearly equally capable. But still prejudice rears its head.

If you look at my photo on the cover of this book, you'll notice that I'm white. I've experienced other forms of harassment, but never racism. I'm a little ashamed to admit that it's only in the last three or four years that I've really started understanding how I benefit from being white. I've never been mistaken for the other white kid in class. I've never been stopped and searched by the police for no reason. I've never had a loan request rejected because of my postcode. I've never had to change my name because someone else decided it was too difficult to say. I've never been turned down for a job because of the colour of my skin. I've never had to overcome the assumption that I wasn't suited to learning at school, university or work.

I've heard people say, "It's not my fault I benefitted from being white! I didn't choose to be born into this situation." And that's true. But neither is it the fault of the BAME person that they weren't born into the kind of privilege I realise I have benefitted from as a white person.

Have you heard of the concept of marginal gains? It's a sports term. Lots of small improvements in technique, preparation or technology add up to a big gain in performance. I think the opposite is true when it comes to discrimination. Privilege isn't so much about advantages as it is the absence of a series of daily disadvantages that, added up, can stop a person thriving in the way we all deserve to. These 'marginal losses' add up to a huge reduction in opportunity.

So, it's desperately important that we have a plan to call out racism and injustice whenever we see it. If we agree that everyone deserves to thrive in life, then we can do something about it. These are hard conversations, and the Kinder Feedback Method can help us get ready to have them.

The powerful BUILD method is especially useful here. BUILD's simple structure makes it easy to get your thoughts straight. The BUILD approach means you're less likely to get into an argument. And the BUILD method means you're more likely to find a resolution.

As I mentioned before, when using BUILD it can be helpful to start with the U. So, let's have a look.

Understand

Understand reminds us to consider what might be going on for the person who did the thing we don't like. Of course, this is understandably harder to do if you've been discriminated against. Your first impulse won't be to imagine what led the other person to this outburst. But by stepping into their shoes, we create some space for empathy. That calms our tone of voice, which is crucial in how others hear us.

We tend to think that people who are being racist are simply racist and that they are purposely discriminating. But it could be unintentional. It might come from a place of ignorance, distraction, or lack of awareness.

Of course, just because they didn't intend harm doesn't make it ok. But some understanding that the harm was not meant can make it easier to resolve. Perhaps they haven't learned yet that we're all biased and need to be on our guard for that. Perhaps their partner is having some hospital tests today so they're distracted. Perhaps their boss has just yelled at them.

And how might it feel to be told that you did something that a colleague, or a friend-of-a-friend, or a contact on social media found harmful and considers racist?

I can tell you from personal experience that it's hard. It's not as hard as being on the receiving end of racism, of course. But when last year I mindlessly recalled a joke from a famous 1980's comedy troupe and one of my kids responded, "Dad, when you say that, it's racist. What are you thinking?" it hit really hard. My first reaction was to reject the accusation. Then my reaction was to justify myself: "I'm not racist; look at my work, you know me." Then to justify the joke. And then to stop and think. On reflection there was a racist trope in there. And eventually I thanked them and apologised.

So, I put the U in BUILD between the B and the I so that it spells BUILD. But that Understanding is helpful right through the BUILD conversation, and especially at the start, perhaps as a way into the conversation.

Let's consider Jamirrudin, who has been asked by his manager if they can call him "Jim – as it would make it so much easier for everyone."

Jamirrudin considers his manager's position for a moment. Perhaps he's been asked by other members of the team. Perhaps he's trying to make it easier for Jamirrudin to get on with his new colleagues. Perhaps because other people use nicknames at work, he doesn't realise how dehumanising this can be. And given all of this it might be hard for his manager to hear that this is a racist request.

"'I'm sure you didn't mean it this way, and I imagine this might be hard to hear."

Jamirrudin is starting from a place of understanding, rather than leading with, "you're racist" (which is an accusation). That's a better place from which to create a kinder conversation.

Behaviours

And so you come to describing their behaviour. The key to talking it out without falling out is to talk about what they did, not what they are.

If you use what they did or said to draw conclusions about what they are, or to guess at their motives, intentions and/or personality traits, they're more likely to disagree. You're more likely to argue, and they're unlikely to change. Try to care less about what they are but instead to hold them accountable for the impact of what they did, their words and actions.

You can do this by describing as accurately and factually as you can what happened. Remember, you're looking to express it in a way that a reasonable person would have to agree it did happen.

"When you ask if you can shorten my name to Jim because it will make things easier for you…"

Impact

The step of describing the impact fully belongs to you. And it's one of the kindest and most generous parts of BUILD feedback, because you are giving something so important but so rarely offered – self-awareness.

How does it feel to be treated in this way? Does it make you feel angry, sad, uncomfortable, marginalised?

"It makes me feel like you are not interested in me as a person, because my name is who I am."

How did those words come across to you? "It felt racist to me."

Listen

You shouldn't have to worry about hurting the feelings of people who say or do racist things. Remember, often people don't intend to do or say something racist, and being told that they did is likely to provoke a response in the other person.

"I'd really like to hear your perspective on this."

So, by listening to them you give them the opportunity to unpack their response, their thinking, their feelings. And evidence shows when you listen with genuine empathy, the other person is more likely to see both sides of the story, more likely to see their weaknesses as well as their strengths, and more likely to see the need to change.

"Can you help me understand your thinking here?"

Do differently

Part of kinder feedback is a desire to help educate and change the attitudes and behaviours of the other person. People aren't fixed in their attitudes. Instead, think of them as learners who want to and are able to learn, grow and change.

We don't give feedback so we can feel justified in our indignation, although we might be within our rights to do so. We're giving the other person a chance to reflect and change so things are better in the future.

Even as kids, we don't like being told what to do. It feels like a telling-off. So, we don't tell the other person what to do. Instead, you can invite them to consider changes for themselves: "What might you do differently?"

You might consider not only what we are against (racism), but what we are for:

"How can we work together to give everyone a fair chance here?"

"I know we all want to make things better; what could we do together?"

Bringing it all together

Jamirrudin has been asked by his manager if they can call him "Jim – as it would make it so much easier for everyone."

He might respond like this:

"I'm sure you didn't mean it this way, and I imagine this might be hard to hear, but when you ask if you can shorten my name to Jim because it will make things easier for you, it makes me feel like you are not interested in me as a person. My name is who I am. And it felt a bit racist to me. Can you help me to understand your thinking here?"

Jamirrudin gives his manager space to reflect and talk here…

"Ok – I hear you. I'm wondering what you'd be happy to do here so things work for everyone?"

Jamirrudin can also add some ideas of his own as part of "what could we do differently."

"Maybe at the next team meeting I can introduce myself and tell people how to pronounce my name. Maybe I could even talk a little about this conversation and how it felt so we can all make things better for people in the future? How does that sound to you?"

OTHER EXAMPLES OF RACISM KINDLY SHARED BY COLLEAGUES

Here are some other examples. You may feel comfortable using the BUILD Kinder Feedback approach to speak up by yourself. But if you feel exposed speaking up by yourself, find allies and speak up together.

Viraj keeps being mistaken for the other person of Asian descent on his floor at work. He isn't sure if it's a genuine mistake or if people might now be turning it into a joke he isn't in on. Here's how he might tackle this…

"I know you probably didn't mean to offend, and I hope you are ok to hear this…

When you mistake me for Nasir – and that's the second time that happened – it makes me feel you aren't seeing me but my race. It makes me sad not being seen as an individual who deserves to be noticed."

"What's your view about what's been happening here?"

Mercy has given a presentation and been congratulated by her boss: "You are actually really articulate, aren't you?" Mercy thought the presentation was ok but no better than her white colleague gave in the previous meeting. What was intended as praise came across as racism. Mercy feels she needs to say something…

"I am acutely aware of this kind of thing because I've experienced it so much. When you congratulate me for being articulate, it makes me feel perhaps you didn't expect me to be for some reason – perhaps the colour of my skin. You may not have meant it this way. I'm interested to hear what your thinking was here.

"Ok, I know we all want to make things better, what could we do together?"

Asha has not been offered a place on a training course, while her two white colleagues have. She feels her manager may not see her as 'leadership material' because of her race. Here's how she might address this.

"This might be a tricky subject, but I think we need to address it. I heard that John and Kate ave been put forward for leadership training. I feel I am just as qualified as them to progress. I'd be grateful if you could explain what's happening here.

"What could we do together so that I can continue to develop?"

Aaliyah's colleague has asked her, "Where are you from, originally?"

"This is hard for me to say, and I imagine it may be hard for you to hear. When you ask me where I am from 'originally', I imagine you're wanting to show interest in me and my background, which is lovely, but it makes me feel like you see me as somehow foreign and that makes me uncomfortable. I am really interested in your perspective on this…

"Ok, I know we all want to make things better, what could we do together?"

Aroha has heard one of her team use a racist word to describe her. She wants to call it out and make it clear it is not acceptable.

"When you use that word to describe me, to me that's a racist word and it makes me so sad and angry to hear it from you. I'd like you not to use that word again, but I'd also like to hear what was happening that led you to say that."

Robert has just heard he didn't get the internal promotion that he interviewed for last week. He feels he is more qualified than the person who did get the job. He's concerned he may be suffering because of the bias that means people from Black, Asian or minority ethnic backgrounds tend to be recruited for experience whilst White people tend to be recruited on potential. He decides to broach the topic with his manager.

"I'm sad to hear that I didn't get that job, as I think I'm suitably qualified and ready for that level of responsibility – and I know it's only my view, but perhaps more qualified than the person who did get the job. This is difficult to talk about, but I just can't pull myself away from the idea it might be because of my race – not consciously on your part, but everyone has biases, and we know it's happened before here. Would you be ok to explore that with me for a bit?"

"Thanks, what might we do differently here so everyone can feel confident they are getting a fair chance?"

THE BYSTANDER EFFECT

You would think that if lots of people witness a racist behaviour then someone is likely to speak out. But evidence shows that the more people are present the less likely it is that anyone will speak up. This is called 'the bystander effect'.

Other studies show people are less likely to speak up if the behaviour is part of cultural norms like banter or hurtful personal jokes.

And if you're a white person you may be worried about the implications for you in calling out racism. But please remember, it's worse for the person on the receiving end of it.

So, it's just as important as bystanders that we have a plan for how we'll respond when we need to. If you are not the subject of racism, you might want to go back and read this chapter again and think about how you would respond to these situations as a bystander.

When you do speak up and act to improve equality for others, it isn't only great for them. It will improve your own wellbeing too. A study showed that someone with high 'inclusiveness activity' is four times more likely to have good wellbeing across all measures, including health, happiness and relationships, than someone who doesn't support equality and diversity.[2]

Speaking up about racism is positive for everyone involved.

Other models talk about 'calling out' behaviour, saying, "Hold on, that's not right." Some models talk about 'calling in', which is asking people to explain, bringing them into a dialogue to build understanding. BUILD Kinder Feedback supports you to do both of these things. You can make clear what is not acceptable and have a conversation about what will make things better.

And we need to make things better.

PART IV

MASTER BUILDER

17

ARE YOU RECEIVING?

Let's go back to my personal bullying experience.

The truth is, I wasn't the one being bullied. I was the one doing the bullying. I have high standards and I felt my colleague was not meeting those. My attempts to direct them, as I told myself I was doing, played out in quite unintended ways.

Remember we talked about how it counts as bullying even if it wasn't intentional? I truly didn't realise I had slipped into bullying them. When I was told, I was mortified. I was so grateful for the feedback. It meant we could work things through. I could apologise properly. And I could learn and change.

There are three things we can learn from this.

First, it's hard for people to speak up. What was stopping that person from speaking up sooner? I suspect fear of my reactions or of causing conflict. It was hard for them to speak up instead of clamming up. I hadn't developed BUILD at that point. If they'd known its simple structure it might have been easier to find the words to show me the impact of my behaviour.

Second, the importance of receiving feedback. If I'd been more open to feedback, what a fantastic opportunity for growth it would have been. I would have learned the impact of my behaviour sooner and taken steps to prevent further damage to our working relationship, and to the team as a whole.

Third, this is an important lesson about impact. We really have very little idea of the impact of our behaviour on others. Even the most self-aware of us actually have very little insight.

It's a hard but important truth that it really could be any of us behaving badly or even bullying another person without realising it.

BUILD helps us to nurture kinder relationships. We can not only be open to feedback, but actively seek it out. Giving feedback is central to the Kinder Feedback Method, of course. But receiving it and even seeking it out are equally important.

Why? What's the benefit to you of getting feedback from the people you work with?

It shows you the impact you're having. You can use BUILD to show people the impact of their behaviour – and they can use it to show you the impact of yours. Without feedback there's no way to know the impact you're having. That means you can't learn or change.

Receiving feedback helps resolve issues that you might not have even been aware of. And as we've seen, a kinder relationship doesn't only impact the two people in it. It has a ripple effect that helps create kinder workplaces, homes and communities.

Being curious about how you land with other people is a great way to learn, get better, and grow.

But let's be honest: It's hard to hear that you've hurt someone else or that your behaviour had a negative impact on them. When someone's giving me feedback, I find this mnemonic helpful to put me in the right state of mind to hear it, and I hope you will too:

I'm Grateful for the Insight, and this Feedback is True for them. Feedback really is a GIFT.

Let's think now about your Chosen Conversation. You might think of other relationships at work and home, too.

Is there something you could actively seek feedback about? You don't have to wait for feedback to come to you. You can ask for it – and chances are the other person will be delighted that you're open to hearing their perspective.

Maybe there's something that, if you're truthful with yourself, you know people can find challenging. Maybe you know you have a tendency to get over-zealous at work and put the pressure on other people to get things done. Or perhaps you're aware that you tend to respond to conflict at home with a solid 'avoid' strategy of passive-aggressive comments.

Could you ask the people around you to help you out by giving you BUILD feedback? You're trying to change – and feedback can help you do that.

Think about the last time someone gave you feedback about a behaviour of yours. How did you react? With indignation?

Annoyance? Brushing it off? Or maybe you were open to it, but you felt ashamed or worried?

How might you have responded if you'd seen it as a GIFT? Think about how you would receive that feedback now you know more about the Kinder Feedback Method.

When we receive a gift, we say thank you. Let's try that with the gift of feedback too. Thanking the person who is giving you feedback takes courage. It's hard to say, "Thank you for showing me how my behaviour impacts you. It gives me a chance to keep improving how I do things. Please do that again if you think it's needed." You'll have noticed that was an ABC of appreciation.

But when you learn to say thank you for feedback, it creates a shift in perspective. Receiving feedback becomes a more positive experience, even if it's also uncomfortable.

Receiving feedback graciously doesn't mean the other person is right. Remember, this isn't about who's right and who's wrong. The Kinder Feedback Method is about reaching agreement and resolution. Maybe they're right, or maybe you've been misunderstood. Either way, feedback gives you insight and new information about the situation. What you do with that information is up to you.

We are only aware of a very small amount of how we come across to others. That makes feedback very valuable! It's a perspective we wouldn't have seen otherwise. But it's still hard to hear sometimes. As well as thinking of feedback as a GIFT, you can try these four steps.

- **Listen**. Give them a chance to fully describe their experience, no matter how tempting it is to jump in and say your piece. Use your level 4 listening skills.
- **Be curious**. This is a new perspective and you might learn a lot from it.
- **Empathise**. Use those empathy muscles we've been BUILDing. Step into their shoes and think about how the situation feels to them.
- **Choose**. You can take their words as an insult, or as feedback.

There are always two sides to a story. If you were giving feedback to someone else using BUILD, your view would be true for you, right? But it might not be true for them. So can you suspend any defensive reactions and respect their view, even if you see it differently?

Carrie had been planning a jam-packed family week over the summer holidays. It was the only week she and her partner could both take off work and they were excited to share it with their kids. Carrie couldn't understand why her teenage son was being so surly about it. She'd shared BUILD with her family after learning it at a workshop, so they agreed to try it out.

Carrie's son told her that she was arranging activities without asking him first, which Carrie admitted was true. Now they were in agreement about her behaviour. He explained that he was excited to have some downtime to play games and hang out with his friends. He wasn't interested in the same things his parents were. Carrie activated her empathy and remembered what it was like to be a teenager and want to hang out with her pals.

Carrie asked what they could do differently to resolve the issue. Her son suggested making time for at least one family outing and several family dinners that week, but also scheduling free time that he could spend how he liked. Everyone had a much smoother and more enjoyable holiday as a result.

It's hard to hear that our actions are causing a problem, but it's also completely human. We're all doing our best, and sometimes we don't see the impact or the other person's point of view. By being open to feedback you open the way for much kinder relationships and give yourself a powerful opportunity for growth, too.

Think again about your Chosen Conversation. Is there anything they might need to give you feedback about that might be helpful to you, if you have some self-awareness and you can be honest with yourself? What might you need to hear? And can you offer them some space to let you know about that?

18

THE THING OR SOMETHING ELSE?

A tea bag. We were rowing about a tea bag. I'm talking a full-on angry argument, all over two square inches of perforated paper and a few fragranced leaves.

I love a nice cup of tea. Anyone who knows me knows that. They also know I'm very fussy about how it's made. It's got to be steeped for just the right time, there must be precisely the right amount of milk, and of course it has to be the right tea. Sort of like Goldilocks, but for a good cuppa.

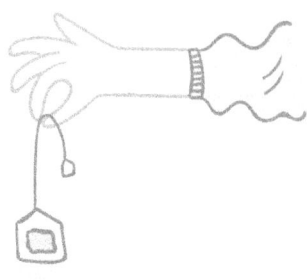

So, I'm standing in my kitchen and my lovely, perfectly made tea in my favourite cup is going cold because I'm too busy having an argument about the tea bag.

You see, I'd left it in the sink, because the bin was full. And I was busy. It's not that important, is it? It's just a tea bag in the sink. Easy to move. I couldn't see what the problem was. So the row raged on until my wife just walked out of the room and I went back to work.

But I still felt bothered. Why would we argue about something so small and insignificant? Leaving the black cloud in the air didn't feel good so I went to my wife and told her I was sorry. That I wouldn't do it again.

All good, right? I took responsibility and apologised, and even pre-emptively answered, "What might you do differently in future?"

Wrong. The answer I got was not what I expected at all.

"You just don't get it, do you? It's not about the tea bag. There's no point talking about it if you can't see the problem."

I was confused. My wife continued.

"It's the same old Student Dad."

Student Dad was one of my wife's nicknames for me. I thought it was affectionate, but it didn't sound very affectionate right then. It started with the rubbish bin (garbage can for some readers!) in the kitchen. When you're busy doing important stuff, there isn't always time to empty it. So sometimes I'd add a bit too much, but if you gave it a good shove down you could fit a lot more in there. It was almost overflowing but not quite – like I might have done in my student days at college.

Ok, I thought. The least I can do is get rid of the offending teabag. So I scooped it out of the sink, still dripping quite strong tea at this point, and carried it over to the bin, which was full to overflowing. The remnants of my lunch were in there… shoved down very nicely, thank you.

See, I thought, with a touch of that self-righteous indignation. I wasn't being unreasonable by leaving the bag in the sink. The bin was just full. But I was all in by now. I tried to drag the plastic sack out, but there was too much shoved in, and it broke. I tried again. It broke again.

It took a good seven minutes of this epic saga to free that bag of garbage. Things kept falling out. I couldn't tie the bag because it had broken so I had to double bag it, which is a Jedi skill all of its own, I can tell you.

By this time I was furious. I was too busy for all this! So I dragged the bag outside, making sure everyone could hear what I was doing and how helpful I was being.

If you're wondering where this saga ends, believe me, so was I. It felt like I'd been wrangling that tea bag all day. I strode back into the kitchen only to realise the teabag had dripped across the worktop and stained the sink. The worktop was an easy fix – I wiped it up. But the stain wouldn't come out of the sink.

KINDER CONVERSATIONS

I took a deep breath and went to ask my wife how best to get the stain off the sink.

"Don't put tea bags in it."

Wow. All that hard work to sort the room out, and I get sarcasm!

Can you see the righteous indignation stacking up here? We all get like that sometimes.

But then it hit me. My wife spent a lot of time in the kitchen. As well as making wonderful meals for our family, it's where she would sit to prepare the yoga classes she taught several times a week. Of course she wanted it to be a nice place to be. She didn't want overflowing rubbish or having to wipe up after me.

It was never about the tea bag. It was about my lack of respect for her environment. My lack of respect for her time.

That's when I realised: sometimes it's not about the thing at all. Sometimes it's about something much more important. So I went back, I apologised, and while I can't say I've never put a tea bag in the sink since, I've not done it often.

If you find yourself irritated about something that 'shouldn't be a big deal' or someone in your life is frustrated and you can't see why it's an issue, remember this tea bag story. Sometimes the problem at hand isn't the problem at all.

Let's think about your Chosen Conversation. Ask yourself, is it about the thing? Or is it about something else? Are you cross because your kids never clean up? Or because it feels like they don't respect you enough to do as you ask?

Are you frustrated that your friend always gets you to buy the first round? Or that they usually leave before the second round so it feels like you're doing all the buying?

Is it really that your colleague microwaved fish in the office microwave? Or are you frustrated because they always take their lunch at the busiest time and leave everyone else to pick up the reins?

Is your Chosen Conversation about a specific action? Or is it really about something else? Trust, respect, the relationship?

Now you know what it's really about, it's easier to figure out what you want from the conversation. To be listened to? To have support during the lunch rush? For your friends to be more considerate?

Use this newfound knowledge to plan how to offer fearlessly gentle feedback for a productive and kind conversation.

19

THE BEST STORYTELLER YOU'VE EVER MET IS...

We all love a good story. Think about your favourite movie or book and how you feel when you're watching or reading it. It's like you're right there, flying that spaceship or solving that clue. You feel every emotion.

Me, I love underdog movies, when someone you wouldn't expect to win out-competes the obvious candidates and wins against all odds: *Hunt for the Wilderpeople; Moneyball; The Pelican Brief.* I can't get enough of them.

Great stories create strong emotions. They have us cheering, crying and laughing. Sometimes the emotions stay long after the credits roll.

But the best storyteller you'll ever encounter isn't Shakespeare or Dickens. It's not Dan Brown and it's not even Steven Spielberg.

The best storyteller you'll ever meet is... you.

You've got a voice in your head, narrating your life, right? Some people experience their inner voice as words, for others it's more about feelings or images. But it's there, piecing together lots of random things happening in the world – most of which have nothing to do with you really – and stitching them into a nice, neat narrative.

And you're the hero at the centre. You're telling a story.

Your story creates your emotions. It makes sense, when you think about it. If a story on the page or screen can have you biting your nails or throwing the book across the room in annoyance (please don't do this if you use an e-reader), how much more powerful is your own story?

But not all stories are true. Your perceptions, biases, hopes and fears colour the story you tell yourself.

Think about that Chosen Conversation. Or you can think of another relationship you'd like to improve, or a disagreement you had recently. Ask yourself this helpful question: What story am I making up about this?

Take a look at the story in your head about the other person, about their intentions, about what they did or didn't do and what it all meant for you, and how that story made you feel.

Maybe you're telling a story where they don't respect you, or they want to make your life difficult, or they don't care about what's important to you. The story is all about you, because that's what the storyteller in our mind does. It tells stories about us.

WHAT STORY AM I MAKING UP ABOUT THIS?

And here's the truth: there are three sides to every story. Their side, your side, and the reality somewhere in the middle.

Use the U step of BUILD on yourself, to think about the stories you're making up. You can step into their shoes and have a guess at what their story might be. Even if you're wrong – and as we talked about, you likely will be – you're still building empathy. You're breaking out of your own story and looking for that middle ground.

Have you ever been angry for longer than ninety seconds? I was angry for two years about those dirty dishes ruining our holiday, causing that argument and the ongoing tension in the kitchen. The chemical component of anger in our systems lasts for just ninety seconds so if you've ever been angry for longer than that, it's because your story kept it going, stoking the fires of anger or disappointment or resentment.

And here's the powerful thing about all of this. If it's just a story you are making up, then the opportunity is open to you to make up a different story. A more helpful story. So you might ask yourself now, what different story could you make up that might just be more helpful?

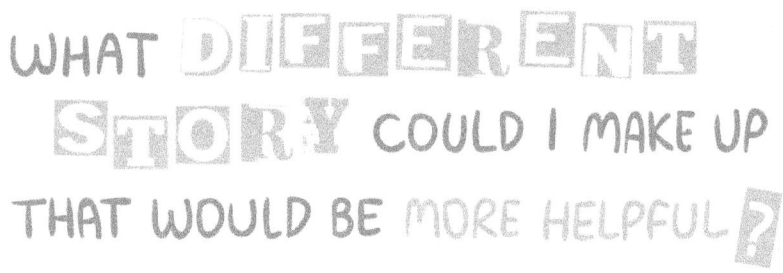

APPRECIATE YOURSELF

There's another part of the Kinder Feedback Method that you can use on yourself, too: The ABCs of appreciation. Remember, people in successful relationships experience five times more praise than criticism. That includes your relationship with yourself.

Let's have a go at using the ABCs of appreciation – on you.

What's something you did recently that's praiseworthy? It doesn't have to be winning a Nobel prize or curing cancer. It could be helping a neighbour with their shopping, showing someone how to do a task they were struggling with at work, cooking your partner their favourite meal… just something that made someone's life a little better.

That's your Action. What was the Benefit to the other person? Or to you?

And how will you find ways to Continue doing that amazing thing you did?

We're all telling ourselves stories all the time. That's not a bad thing. But being aware of those stories will help you separate out what's happening from what you're telling yourself about it. You can think more consciously about how you would like the story to end and how you can use the Kinder Feedback Method to help you get there.

20

MOVING PAST THE FEAR OF GIVING FEEDBACK

If you've ever so much as thought about trying to give someone feedback about their behaviour, you know how nerve-racking it can feel.

Let's talk about that for a moment. And we need to start by talking about biases. I am biased, of course. But then, so are you. We're all subject to all kinds of biases that lead us to make irrational decisions.

Biases are mental shortcuts that are designed to save the brain time and energy. That sounds great! But most of our biases evolved tens of thousands of years ago, to keep us safe from saber-toothed tigers, club-wielding rivals, and living in dangerous conditions.

They're not that suited to modern living.

A bias that often shows its face when we need to make a decision is called loss aversion. We all hate losing about three times more than we like winning. That's why you'll stay in line long after the queue has started moving, because you invested time in that line and you don't want your time to have been wasted.

It's why in the financial markets, people will hold on to a stock that's falling in value for three times longer than it takes them to sell a winning stock that's gone up in value. It's why we stick in jobs we hate, relationships that don't work for us, and friendships we've outgrown. Because we've invested in them.

We're often scared to speak up because we've invested in that relationship (be it romantic, familial, friendship, or work). We don't want to lose.

But ask yourself this. What might you gain by speaking up?

When someone does something that doesn't work for you, that you find hurtful, or that damages the relationship, it's important to speak up. When someone does something that holds back a project, or harms someone else, it's important to speak up.

But speaking up can feel hard. Even with tools like the ABCs and BUILD in your back pocket, it can be a challenge to find the right words. Why is that? The answer is a simple four-letter word: Fear. It's a bit like bungee jumping or walking a tightrope. It's a step into the unknown, and that's scary. You don't know if you'll manage to speak up without messing up. You fear their reactions or possible repercussions.

All these are really about fear for our safety.

No matter what the situation, it's the boat we're used to sailing in. And the thought of rocking the boat is scary.

We are evolutionarily wired for safety. Remember fight or flight? When we're afraid, 10% of the blood in our brains drains to our body. We don't need to think. We need to fight or flee. So here we are facing an important conversation, and our brain is busy shutting down higher order thinking, creativity, problem solving, and language skills, all things that would have been so very useful!

And you know what comes next: avoid or attack. Avoidance means fleeing from the conversation. We say nothing, or we skirt around the issue. We minimise it, sugar coat it, or water it down. These are all forms of avoidance.

Or we go into attack mode. Now we come out fighting! We're determined to be right, and we want to force our views and compel them to change. We challenge their motivations and question their values. Here comes that self-righteous indignation.

Neither of these approaches work.

The Kinder Feedback Method helps you get past what isn't working so you can talk together about what will work better for both of you. But for the method to be effective, you need to actually give the kinder feedback! And that means getting past the fear response.

Thankfully there is an easy way to move past the fear. Three ways in fact: breathe, brain, and bravery.

First, **breathe**. Just breathe. Science has shown that the quickest way to get from fight or flight back to calm is to take three really big, deep breaths. Try it now. Make them as deep and long as you can manage.

Second, **brain**. You need to switch your brain back on again and get the energy flowing there so you can think about what to say. The quickest way to do this is to ask a question that takes some thought. You can use the U step of BUILD for this: "I wonder what's going on for them right now? What might they be thinking or feeling?" This brings your brain back online. And you're creating empathy.

Third, **bravery**. Fortune favours the brave. If you're not feeling brave, you can trick your brain into thinking you are. All you need to do is tell yourself that you are brave, and about all the wonderful benefits of that bravery. "I am brave enough to do this because it will improve our relationship." "I am brave enough to do this because I know they don't want to have this impact on me – I am helping them."

The three Bs - Breathe, Brain, and Bravery help you calm down, get out of attack or avoid mode, and move forward.

You're not the only one who's afraid

Receiving feedback is difficult, too. It's not easy to hear that you didn't have the impact you wanted, or that you caused harm or distress to someone else. After all, you're doing your best, just as we all are.

No one likes to feel judged, and critical feedback can feel judgemental. They might worry about the relationship, their work prospects, or whether they might lose face.

They fear for their safety. Their brain is telling them to fight or flee. Avoid or attack. Maybe they deflect the blame. "It's not my fault!" The shutters come down. Nobody's home. Or maybe they attack right back. They inflate their own self-righteous bubble of indignation. The temperature is rising, and out come all the justifications. You can't resolve anything from here.

The Kinder Feedback Method is designed to lower the temperature. You can use the steps of BUILD to separate facts from impacts. You can describe behaviour in a factual, provable way. It makes it easier to get to a point of agreement.

When you practise understanding – asking what might be going on for them – you can also take a moment to notice their body language. Do they look like they might be about to avoid or attack?

Level 4 listening brings the temperature down further by giving space for them to talk.

But what else can you do to help the other person's fear? Try these three simple steps: tempo, tone, and together. What's great is that each of these actions is triggered by the three Bs you already did: breathe, brain, and bravery.

Tempo. By slowing down what you say and giving space between your sentences, you calm both yourself and the other person. And you'll already be doing this if you took those three deep breaths.

Tone. This is even easier. By stepping into their shoes to switch your brain back on, you raised your empathy levels. That automatically softens your tone of voice and makes you feel like less of a threat.

Together. Show them you have their interests in mind as well as your own. You are being brave for both of you and helping them feel safer. You do this by choosing words that show you're in it together. Can we talk? Let's find a way we can work through this together.

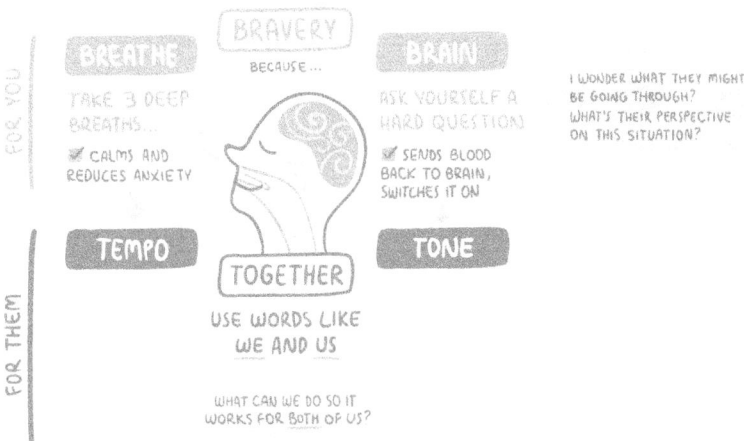

Kofi had had enough of arguing with his dad about their upcoming family party. Dad had agreed to take care of the snacks, but the party was approaching fast and no snacks were forthcoming. Kofi didn't want the guests having only cereal and crackers all night, but he was too busy to sort it out himself. So, Kofi tried BUILD.

Behaviour: You agreed to take care of the snacks for the party.

Understand: Maybe his dad was busy at work.

Impact: I'm concerned our guests won't have anything to eat.

Listening: What's happening here?

So far so good, right? But when they reached the L, his dad crossed his arms, glared, and said he didn't want to talk about it.

Kofi felt nervous to try again, not wanting another stony silence. But rather than fix the snacks himself while grumbling, like he might have done before The Kinder Feedback Method, Kofi tried breathe, brain, and bravery. He took a deep breath and thought more about his father's reaction. The crossed arms and crosser tone told Kofi his dad felt defensive. So he tried again, letting empathy soften his tone and language.

Do differently: "Can we talk? Let's find a way we can work through this together."

Kofi's dad agreed to talk, and admitted he felt overwhelmed. Several guests had specific dietary allergies and he wasn't certain if some snacks were off limits. They agreed to go through the guest list and email those people, to be sure they could provide safe snacks for them to enjoy.

When you work through your fear of giving feedback, and reduce their fear too, you start to create the safety you both need to have a meaningful discussion. Now you can hear each other's point of view and find ways to do things differently to build an even stronger relationship.

21

SERENDIPITY

You remember where we started, with a pile of dirty dishes? Well, as luck would have it, I was given the chance to revisit the situation after I developed BUILD, and after I had rehearsed it with my groups. I was able to find out for myself what a difference BUILD made to a situation that had once caused a family blow-up.

The situation was almost an identical repeat of the first incident. We came home to find another tower of dirty dishes, piled in the sink.

This time though, I knew all I had to do was use BUILD. Two statements, two questions. I described the behaviour. "There are dirty dishes in the sink." There were indeed dirty dishes in the sink. It was a statement of fact we could all agree with.

I sought to understand. I thought perhaps my kids had been called away for some reason, or just lost track of time. I kept that in mind as I described the impact: "It makes me feel like you don't care about our home environment. It feels like our homecoming is ruined."

Then I asked the question, "What was happening here?" and I listened to their answer.

My kid confided that one of their friends had had a bad mental health day. They'd gone to keep their friend company.

This was a case where the second question was unnecessary. I didn't ask, "What could we do differently?" because I wouldn't want them to do anything differently. They'd gone to support a friend.

The B-U-I-L steps were enough to help me understand the situation and resolve it without conflict.

And imagine how awful I would have felt if I'd attacked or avoided, and then found out later how wonderful they had been. And how using BUILD in this way built our relationship.

Yet of course any situation provides an opportunity to learn, so I finished BUILD with the D and asked, "Is there anything I could do to support you here?"

"You could dry, while I wash," they said as they threw me the tea-towel with a smile.

Now you know the Kinder Feedback Method, you can keep it in your back pocket as a tool for whenever you need to have a conversation that might have seemed difficult before, and you can see now can be so much easier than you thought. Read this book as often as you need to and practise the techniques so they become second nature.

Use them at home, at work, and with friends, to build a life supported by kinder, gentler, more productive conversations.

REFERENCES

2. REPAIRING RELATIONSHIPS

1. Holt-Lunstad J, Smith TB, Layton JB (2010) *Social Relationships and Mortality Risk: A Meta-analytic Review.* PLoS Med 7(7): e1000316
2. The Harvard Study of Adult Development

3. THE ABC OF APPRECIATION

1. Gottman J M, Coan, J, Carrerre S, Swanson C (1998) *Predicting Marital Happiness and Stability from Newlywed Interactions* University of Washington
2. Workhuman (2011) *Globoforce Mood Tracker*
3. I heard this study being quoted on the Radio 4 Today Programmes sometime in 2013 but I can't find the study online now, but I promise it's a real study!
4. OC Tanner Performance: Accelerated. A New Benchmark for Initiating Employee Engagement, Retention and Results
5. Workhuman (2012) *Globoforce Mood Tracker*
6. Zenger J, Folkman J (2013) *The Ideal Praise-to- Criticism Ration* Harvard Business Review

    Fredrickson, (2013) *Updated Thinking on Positivity Ratios.* American Psychologist

    Gottman J M (1993) *What Predicts Divorce?: Relationship Between Marital Processes and Marital Outcomes.* Psychology Press

    Newburg, Waldman (2012) *Words Can Change Your Brain: 12 Conversation Strategies to Build Trust, Resolve Conflict, and Increase Intimacy.* Plume

    Achor (2012) *Positive Intelligence* Harvard Business Review

    Wang, Shen, Xu, Liu, Ma, Zhao, Fu, Pan, Feng and Li (2008) *Negative Words on Surgical Wards Result in Therapeutic Failure of Patient-controlled Analgesia and Further Release of Cortisol After abdominal Surgeries.* Minerva Anestesiologica
7. Williams L A, Bartlett M Y (2014) *Warm Thanks: Gratitude Expression Facilitates Social Affiliation in New Relationships via Perceived Warmth..* Emotion

REFERENCES

DOI: 10.1037/emo0000017
8. Xing S, Gao X, Jiang Y, Archer M, Liu X.(2018) *Effects of Ability and Effort Praise on Children's Failure Attribution, Self-Handicapping, and Performance* Frontiers in Psychology
9. Lambert N M (2008) *The Role of Appreciation in Close Relationships: A Journal Study* Florida State University Libraries

4. IF WE SAY NOTHING, NOTHING'S GOING TO CHANGE

1. Riskin A (2015) *Impact of incivility on patient safety and clinical performance - The Impact of Rudeness on Medical Team Performance: A Randomized Trial,* Pediatrics
2. Katz D, Blasius K, Isaak R, Lipps J, Kushelev M, Goldberg A, Fastman J, Marsh B, DeMaria S *Affiliations Expand* DOI: 10.1136/bmjqs-2019-009598

10. LISTEN UP

1. Singh Ospina, N (2018) *Eliciting the Patient's Agenda- Secondary Analysis of Recorded Clinical Encounters,* Journal of General Internal Medicine DOI: 10.1007/s11606-018-4540-5
2. Itzachokov G, Kluger N (2018) *The power of listening in helping people change* Harvard Business Review
3. Foulk, Trevor, Woolum, Andrew, Erez, Amir (2016) *Catching rudeness is like catching a cold: The contagion effects of low-intensity negative behaviors* Journal of Applied Psychology, Vol 101(1)

15. BUILD FOR EVERY SITUATION

1. The price of incivility. Porath C, Pearson C. Harv Bus Rev. 2013 Jan-Feb; 91(1-2);114-21, 146 (Accessed 26/04/2019 at https://hbr.org/2013/01/the-price-of-incivility)
2. Gallup, The State of the American Manager, 2015
3. Syed M (2015) *Black Box Thinking,* John Murray Publishing

4. Namie G, (2012) *Health effects of bullying* Workplace Bullying Institute, Impact of workplace bullying on individuals' health

16. SPEAKING UP ABOUT RACISM

1. Rupa Banerjee J G, Oreopoulos R P, (2017) *Do large employers treat racial minorities more fairly?* A new analysis of Canadian field experiment data, University of Toronto
2. Ben C Fletcher, Diversity and Inclusiveness Is Good For Your Wellbeing, Psychology Today UK, 18/9/2016

www.ingramcontent.com/pod-product-compliance
Lightning Source LLC
Chambersburg PA
CBHW070040230426
43661CB00034B/1442/J